Prime Time

MANAGING YOUR MONEY

Prime Time

Building Wealth In Your 40s & 50s

Stoddart

Published in 1998 by Stoddart Publishing Co. Limited
34 Lesmill Road, Toronto, Canada M3B 2T6
Toll-free tel. for Ontario & Quebec: 1-800-387-0141
Toll-free tel. for all other provinces & territories: 1-800-287-0172
Fax: (416) 445-5967 Email: customer.service@ccmailgw.genpub.com

Produced for Investors Group by Alpha Media™
151 Bloor St. W., Suite 890, Toronto, Canada M5S 1S4

02 01 00 99 98 1 2 3 4 5

Canadian Cataloguing in Publication Data

Main entry under title:

Prime time: building wealth in your 40s & 50s

(The Investors Group series)
ISBN 0-7737-5948-4

1. Saving and investment. 2. Middle aged persons — Finance, Personal.
I. Investors Group. II. Series

HG179.P74 1998 332.024'0564 C97-932569-2

JACKET AND TEXT DESIGN: Adele Webster/ArtPlus Limited
PAGE MAKE-UP: Heather Brunton/ArtPlus Limited
COVER ILLUSTRATION: Riccardo Stampatori

Printed and bound in Canada

The information contained in this publication is presented as a general source of information only and is not intended as a solicitation or recommendation to buy or sell specific investments, nor is it intended to provide legal advice. Prospective investors should review the annual report, simplified prospectus, and annual information form of a fund carefully before making an investment decision. No representations are made as to the accuracy of the information contained herein and individuals should consult their professional advisor for advice based on their specific circumstances.

About Investors Group

Investors Group is a Canadian leader in providing personal financial services through financial planning, a unique family of mutual funds, and a comprehensive range of other investment products and services including retirement savings plans, insurance, mortgages, and GICs.

The Investors Group story began in 1940, and we have grown to serve close to one million clients from coast to coast through a dedicated and professional sales force. At the heart of our efforts is a simple, long-term strategy — to work closely with clients to understand their current circumstances and investment preferences and help them achieve their long-term personal and financial goals.

Investors Group is a member of the Power Financial Corporation group of companies.

Acknowledgments

This book was the result of a collaboration among people at three companies. Susan Yates and Arnold Gosewich at Alpha Media initiated and co-ordinated the project. At Investors Group, a large and dedicated team of Chartered Financial Planners, accountants, lawyers, and investment specialists provided tax and financial planning information, as well as general direction on appropriate strategies for consumers in each life stage. At Colborne Communications Centre, Greg Ioannou, Sasha Chapman, and Michael Redhill co-ordinated the writing, editing, and indexing.

About This Book

Prime Time is a book for people who want to take control of their financial lives by learning the principles of investing and money management. You'll find that many of the examples in this book are geared toward people between the ages of 40 and 65, but this range is only a guideline. *Prime Time* is for intermediate investors of all ages. It will equip you to think more clearly and usefully about your own situation and will arm you with questions you can ask to help you reach your dreams. This book is not written as a "do it yourself" guide. In fact, many of the subjects discussed involve complex legal, financial, and tax issues that have been simplified to make them more approachable.

Because the details of each life are different, it would be impossible to cover all of life's possibilities in one place. Readers are urged to seek professional advice on their personal circumstances.

About This Series

Prime Time is the second book in a four-part series designed to help different groups of people take control of their financial lives. The other three books are:

Starting Out, for beginning investors;

Retire Ready, for investors who already have retired; and

Small Business, a book designed to address the special investment needs of the small business owner.

Contents

CHAPTER 1

Retirement Is Closer Than You Think

You, Your Dreams, and Retirement

Freedom. Opportunity. Dreams. That's what financial planning is all about. And now that retirement is right around the corner (instead of on the horizon), it's time to actively start dreaming of a different kind of future. But those dreams have a price tag. Maybe you want to retire early. Maybe you want to buy a summer home. As soon as your working life draws to a close, there will be a whole bundle of things you'll want to do. Whatever you imagine for yourself, it's time to make your money go further by managing it better. Even if you're basically "doing things properly," we think you'll learn a trick or three from this book.

The Big Secret

Personal finance is not really a cold-blooded, penny-pinching exercise in dollar signs and decimal points. In fact, it's a warm and human activity, because it's all about reaching your dreams. Managing your money allows you to get more bang for every buck — and that means you can say yes to yourself more often and more generously. Yes to you, to your goals, and to the life you want to live. The fact that you're reading this book shows that you want to make the best possible life for yourself. Everyone deserves personal and family financial independence, and has the ability to achieve it. Add common sense, awareness of your key goals, and a willingness to strengthen some money-building habits, and you're on your way.

Good and Not-So-Good Times

Self-reliance has never been more important. Everything tells us that we're going to have to depend on ourselves more and on others less, whether they're companies or governments. Downsizing, outsourcing, and flattening of hierarchies are now part of the corporate culture. No one these days expects to stick with the same firm, stepping up, perhaps modestly but dependably, through bigger titles and salaries until retirement at age 65. Instead, you are probably making your own career ladder, which includes a variety of workplaces (including stints of self-employment) and frequent reinventions of what you do. Meanwhile, the government social safety net has been shrinking. In general, it's harder to qualify for benefits, the benefits are smaller, and you have to make larger contributions. This makes planning for your retirement more important than ever. And because Canadians are living longer, you not only have to look after yourself better, you'll have to do it for a longer time. So financial planning really is for you. Take charge of your money, and it will cushion the bad times and make the good ones better. It will help you get where you want to go in comfort.

WHAT EXACTLY IS FINANCIAL PLANNING ANYWAY?

Financial planning is:

- preparing for retirement;
- minimizing tax;
- using debt and credit effectively;
- preparing for unexpected financial obligations;
- protecting yourself and your family against loss of income, either through death or disability; and
- being able to earn better returns from your investments with acceptable risk.

Financial planning essentially means paying attention to the money you have today and planning for your future.

Midlife, Without the Crisis

When you were younger and more naive, you probably expected that once you hit your forties you'd have it made — like your parents, you'd own a house, two cars in the driveway, go to work each day at a secure, high-paying job, and take the family on annual vacations to Europe. Sometimes reality can stray far from your daydreams, though. Now that you are better established, you may have a well-paying job, but somehow may still have less disposable income than you did in your twenties or thirties. You may still be paying off the mortgage, funding your children's education, paying for some form of care for your aging parents, and trying somehow to contribute enough to your RRSPs so that at least you can enjoy a stress-free retirement. But you shouldn't have to wait until 65 to enjoy financial well-being. If you already have a financial plan, pull it out and see if it still fits you. And if you don't have one, it's never too late to start.

Taking Charge of Your Financial Life

Your financial plan will be as individual as your fingerprints because it has to fit you — your goals and your circumstances. But the basic components are common to all successful financial approaches, and they are reassuringly simple. The key is to identify the major lifestyle goals, set financial goals to match, and then work out financial strategies that will get you there. So start with information and then apply it.

- First, plan your retirement. All other goals should be planned in the context of what you need to do to ensure a retirement that is free from financial worry.
- Identify your most important short-term goals, those that apply over the next five years. Then set out your longer-term ones, say for the next 10 or 20 years. List them in order of importance.
- Make a habit of becoming aware of your resources, your present and future needs. Be prepared to adjust your goals if necessary.
- Learn to organize. Investments, taxes, wills, and loans are examples of different categories of your financial life. The ability to assess your current situation depends on your ability to keep it all straight.
- Calculate whether you'll be able to put aside enough money to meet your goals in the time you've set to achieve them. You will have to make some changes now if you aren't putting enough away for your retirement.

FIVE STEPS TOWARDS FINANCIAL INDEPENDENCE

1. Set your financial goals for retirement:
   - Figure out what you want to do and how much it will cost
   - Decide where you want to live
   - Determine what sources of income you will have
   - Calculate how much capital you have and how much you will need
   - Set up investment plans to get you there
2. Develop or fine tune your investment strategy:
   - Save up for emergencies (minimum three months' income)
   - Tailor your investment strategy/risk level to your life stage
   - Assess your investment performance at least once a year
   - "Pay yourself first" by investing 10% of what you earn each month
3. Manage your debt and expenses:
   - Get cash flow under control
   - Stay on top of debt and pay off your highest cost debt first
   - Pay off debts before you retire
4. Minimize your taxes:
   - Know all tax deductions, credits, and strategies available to you
   - Maximize your RRSP contribution every year
   - If you haven't already, start contributing to an RRSP — it is never too late
5. Protect yourself:
   - Match your insurance to your needs (make sure you have enough disability coverage to replace any lost income before you retire)
   - Make sure your family will remain financially secure if you or your spouse die

Giving Yourself a Good Life

Living the good life is more than just spending on the things that you enjoy. It is also giving yourself freedom from the stress of worrying how you will keep a roof over your head. You'll never be able to predict when accidents will happen, such as breaking down on the highway or losing your job, but you can prepare for these inevitable difficulties. Putting away a percentage of your earnings each month in a designated emergency account can soften the blow. The last thing you want to do right before retirement is find yourself unemployed or with unexpected major expenses eating away at the money you had saved for your golden years. And although credit cards are great for short-term loans, putting huge expenses on them that you don't expect to be able to pay off by the due date will just add to your financial troubles. So establish a separate fund before problems appear. It's a vital part of financial planning.

THE BASIC PHILOSOPHY

At least once a year, assess your financial situation, as well as your long-term and short-term financial goals. Establish a realistic and comfortable plan to achieve those goals. Implement your plan, and stick with it. You don't need to know everything yourself. Use a financial advisor the same way you would use a doctor — take advantage of the expertise to ensure your financial health.

The Big Three Principles

For the greatest possible financial strength as you build your life, follow these three simple principles:

1. Start planning and rehearsing for life in retirement.
2. Pay off high-cost, non-deductible debts first.
3. Minimize your taxes by using all available deductions, credits, and strategies.

It may not be glamorous, but, over time, these principles are incredibly powerful. The trick is to work out how to stay faithful to them as you make your way through the surprises and changes of life. That's where you'll need to devise strategies and systems, make tradeoffs, juggle priorities, and the like. But if you keep focused on the three principles, many other choices become clearer. The principles will be discussed in more detail later in the book.

WHAT'S YOUR FINANCIAL HEALTH?

GOOD SIGNS

- You know your net worth.
- You know when you want to retire, where you want to live, and what you'll do when you get there.
- You've set up a regular savings program to ensure you steadily direct money toward those goals — nothing fancy, just something that suits you and your goals.
- You've protected yourself against disaster with an emergency fund and an insurance policy.
- You plan to pay off all your debts by the time you retire.
- You know how much you spend today and how that will change in retirement.
- You're maxing out your RRSP. If you took money out to buy a house, you've replaced it in time to avoid paying tax.
- Your will is current and your beneficiaries are current on all your RRSPs and life insurance policies.
- You always save enough for tax time and emergencies.
- You and your spouse share details about the family finances so that either of you can carry on if necessary.

BAD SIGNS

- You're living from paycheque to paycheque, ignoring the fact that many of your peers are being downsized.
- You've had children and/or remarried, but never updated your will.
- You're not sure what you want to do when you retire. You'll figure that out if and when you get there.
- You're gaining debt using credit cards and loans, and maybe even skipping debt payments. The total is growing, not shrinking.
- You used your emergency fund to buy a boat.
- You can't afford to max out your RRSP; you may have even taken money out of your RRSP for a house and never paid it back.
- You can't afford your yearly tax bill.
- Only one of you looks after the finances — and it isn't you.
- You've decided that you don't need disability insurance.

GOOD VS BAD DEBT

Your parents may have told you that all debt is bad, but that's not always true.

Good debt: This is debt that works for you, building your assets, such as borrowing to max out your RRSP. Some types of debt are even tax deductible.

Bad debt: This is debt you acquire through overspending, such as borrowing for that wine tour in France in addition to your annual winter escape. High-cost debt is also bad debt. The worst kind of bad debt is the kind you rack up on your credit card!

LIFE EXPECTANCY

If you are a healthy, non-smoking Canadian between 45- and 55-years-old, you can expect to live into your early eighties. This means that even if you retire as late as age 65, which fewer people are doing these days, your retirement fund will have to last you at least 15 years. If you retire at 55, you will need enough income to last you 25 years, almost as long as you worked! Of course, people cannot predict how long they'll live, but when it comes to providing for retirement years, optimism is also pragmatism.

Yesterday, Today, and Tomorrow

You may have less time and more responsibilities than people just starting out in their financial lives, but you also have greater resources, a clearer sense of your priorities, and lots of motivation. Whatever your age, stage, and financial resources, financial planning will let you make more of what you have. Today you're living with the results of yesterday. Use today to create a tomorrow that is closer to your dreams.

But the most important aspect of this financial planning, like exercise, is to start! It doesn't matter how close you are to retiring — even if you're starting only now, there's still time to make your finances work for you. You don't ever want to look back on these years with regret that you should have done something, anything, for your retirement.

NO MORE YO-YO FINANCIAL PLANNING!

- Think about your retirement goals, and build in activities now that will safeguard them.
- Kick the starvation-diet approach, and start enjoying yourself. Starvation — financial or otherwise — doesn't work. A common-sense approach does.
- Make financial awareness part of your daily lifestyle.
- Prepare a financial plan, stick to it, and monitor your results.
- Remember: every healthy diet includes treats; just don't overindulge.
- Don't be afraid to ask! You wouldn't do your own surgery or defend yourself in court. Professional advisors working with a reputable firm can help you plan and achieve your goals and answer your questions.

PLAN, PLAN, PLAN

Solid finances means a solid lifestyle. Start taking greater control of your finances. You can do this by planning. Pre-authorized payment plans, investment plans, and retirement plans all mean greater lifestyle flexibility in the long-run.

You and the Experts

Many experts are out there to advise you, explain things to you, and provide you with products and services. They range from bankers to stock brokers, financial advisors, accountants, portfolio managers, insurance agents, and lawyers. Some will charge fees, but some advisors provide advice free of charge, since they are paid by financial companies, just as travel agents are paid by transportation and holiday package companies. Choose your financial expert the same way that you would pick your doctor or dentist. Friends' recommendations can help, but also check credentials and follow your instincts. You need to find someone you feel comfortable with and trust. The time to start looking is now. The longer you can work together, the more useful the advisor can be for you.

No matter how carefully you pick and how confident you are in your "normal" life, you may feel tongue-tied when you sit down with the financial expert. Here's how to get the best from the meeting:

- Do your homework. Fill in any forms you've been given in advance, take any papers you have been asked to supply, and write out the questions you want answered during the meeting. Be prepared to provide details of all your family finances. It may make you uncomfortable at first, but advisors need all the information to do the best job for you.
- Expect the expert to have done his or her homework as well. Is the person ready for the meeting? Familiar with your file and background material? Equipped with everything needed to carry out the day's agenda?
- Listen carefully. Ask questions whenever you want more information, or when you don't understand what your advisor is saying. Don't be intimidated! It's not up to you to guess — it's up to the expert to be clear. Professionals will welcome your questions because they want you to understand. Be suspicious of those who brush you off.
- Take notes. Things that seem clear at the time may become blurred in your memory later.
- Cover every topic that was on your list, but don't waste time. Check to see if you are being charged by the hour, but even if you're not, it's courteous to stay on topic.
- Do any necessary follow-up, and make sure that the expert does too.

Above all, remember that the decisions are ultimately up to you. It's your life and your money. Experts can advise and help, but you are in charge. This is a responsibility, as well as a right.

THERE'S NO TIME LIKE THE PRESENT

Now's the time to look at how your assets are working for you so that you can maximize your pre-retirement wealth building.

FILE IT!

If you haven't already, set up a filing system. (If you have, now's your chance to clean it out, and maybe even create a few new files.) If you haven't already discovered how addictive filing is, now's your chance. You'll gain immense satisfaction when you need a piece of paper and can put your finger on it instantly. Do this with your spouse or adult children so that there are no unsolved mysteries in the event of your death.

Buy a two- or four-drawer metal filing cabinet. Use a folder (or your safety deposit box for valuable papers) for each of the following categories:

Statements from Financial Institutions A separate folder for each account.

Credit Card(s) The receipts and statements for each in a separate folder.

Investments Folders for such things as RRSPs and mutual funds.

Home Several folders for documents pertaining to purchase and mortgage (or rent receipts), property tax, repairs, and improvements.

Car Folders for financing, bill of sale, repairs.

Income Tax and Tax-Deductible Items One folder for your previous year's tax form and notice of assessment, and one for all the tax slips and receipts for the current tax year.

Insurance A folder for each kind of insurance (e.g., auto, home, life, disability).

Pension Plan Yearly summaries and other documents from your employer.

Personal Papers Your birth certificate, social insurance card, marriage or divorce papers, passport, will, and other important papers.

Salary Paycheque stubs and any other job-related documents.

Self-Employment Records If you're self-employed, keep a list of invoices rendered. You'll likely need folders for each type of deductible expense.

Warranties, Receipts, Instruction Manuals Keep these for all purchases, both large and small. These may not be part of your financial plan, but they certainly make life easier when kept in one place.

Summary

Retirement is the biggest project most of us undertake in life. To live the way you want, you have to be prepared. Before you rush out to max your RRSP or start an automatic savings plan, ask yourself a few questions that will keep the rest of your financial planning on track:

- What do I need to provide myself with the retirement lifestyle I want?
- What do I have to do to meet those needs?
- Do I know enough about taxes, investments, and strategies to do this without a professional advisor?
- How can I match my healthy saving (and spending) habits with my lifestyle and financial goals?
- Am I prepared for the unexpected?

Don't forget to assess your financial situation at least once a year, or to reassess your long-term and short-term financial goals. Establish a realistic and comfortable plan to achieve those goals. Then, it's just a question of getting to it — after all, the plan's no good if it's only a plan!

ONE MORE TIME

The Big Three Principles:

- ✔ **Start planning and rehearsing for life in retirement.**
- ✔ **Pay off high-cost, non-deductible debts first.**
- ✔ **Minimize your taxes by using all available deductions and credits.**

CHAPTER 2

Making Plans

Whether or not you've thought about it, you probably have a conscious (or unconscious) financial plan. But how do you begin to give that plan some direction? Or reassess it when your circumstances change, as they are about to? After all, you're probably making a lot more money now than you were when you were in your twenties. Your family may now be double income, but it may also have double the expenses. How do you adjust your expectations to fit your changing situation? Let's take a look at some typical situations.

Maggie

Maggie, 51, just celebrated the final payment on her car loan (she couldn't resist buying the Jeep), which had been a drain on her income as a graphic designer. She figures she's been averaging about $56,000 a year for the last few years. Maggie's income is still somewhat irregular — contracts come either not at all or in battalions — but at last she can start throwing some more money at her RRSP. She has a sixteen-year-old daughter who needs glasses, clothing and schoolbooks. Maggie is the only support; she is seriously wondering how to provide for her child's future without mortgaging her own.

Gord and Shelly

Gord, 60, and Shelly, 53, are a double income family. Gord is a personnel manager at a marketing firm, and Shelly is a computer analyst. They have two children, but only one education left to pay for, since the eldest is articling at a law firm and preparing to move out on her own. Gord and Shelly still have a few more years left on their mortgage payments, but Gord's insurance premiums seem to rise almost daily as he continues to chain-smoke. As the personnel manager at his firm, he is all too aware of the trend in downsizing, and although his job has been secure, Gord is starting to worry that he might be next. Their combined income is about $92,000, but Gord and Shelly's investments are scattered and need to be reassessed.

Beth and John

Beth, 45, and John, 47, have four children; the eldest just left for university. For the last 10 years Beth's $110,000 income as a senior partner in a legal firm has been nearly double John's $58,000 as a tenured university professor. Unfortunately, John has always handled their six-figure income in an absent-minded-professor sort of way. Beth and John own a house, a summer home and two cars, but they don't know their personal financial situations, or whether their dream of retiring at age 55 to travel the world and volunteer for a good cause will be possible. Beth also has a mother in chronic care, likely for a good 10 years yet. Beth and John need a financial plan to claim the future as their own.

The Future Begins in the Present

Maggie, Gord and Shelly, and Beth and John all feel frustrated and uncertain about their situations. They don't feel fully in control of where they are, or where they are going. You may be feeling exactly the same way. Given the current unpredictability of the job market and rapid changes taking place, how can anyone predict his or her own financial future?

Although no one can give you the financial-planning equivalent of a crystal ball, there are ways to figure out what your various options are and what's possible for you. The trick is to start by figuring out where you are today.

The Big Picture

This book will take you through a simple, logical series of steps to organize your financial life.

Step 1 Determine your life goals. It is impossible to plan unless you know what you are aiming for.

Step 2 Determine your net worth. That is, find out where you are starting.

Step 3 Find out how much you'll need to have in order to finance your life goals.

Step 4 Calculate your current income, and look to see what you are spending it on. Using a simple expense diary will make it easy. Keep track of your income and expenses for two months.

Step 5 Prepare a budget that will let you live in comfort today while ensuring you are saving enough to meet your goals.

Step 1: Determine Your Life Goals

Only you can identify your life goals and priorities. Do this first: everything else depends on it. Once you know what's most important in your life, you decide on the financial goals and strategies that will let you shape the life you want.

If you haven't already, now's the time to start thinking about what kind of life you want to be living when you leave work for the last time. You've spent your life up to now thinking about this future, and now it's almost here. The goals are a little different now: the focus isn't so much on socking money away for the future, but on figuring out how best to use that nest-egg you've been creating. It might be hard to be specific right now, but it's important to develop a sense of what you believe you'll want and need. Here are some of the kinds of things you might want to be doing:

- maintaining your pre-retirement standard of living
- travelling
- working, consulting — or continuing your education
- buying a vacation/second home
- leaving an inheritance
- doing volunteer work or donating to charities
- taking up long-abandoned hobbies
- learning new sports, such as golf, skiing, sailing — these can be costly

The first of these goals is probably the most pressing: you don't want the end of your work life to be the beginning of diminishing returns. This is where your RRSP will figure in the most.

Depending on your age and how long you plan to work, it may still be decades before you plan to retire. Between now and then you will surely have some non-retirement goals that you want to reach. These goals might be moving into a larger house, buying a second car, or acquiring a lakefront vacation property. Remember to earmark some of your savings for these interim goals, and enjoy yourself while also saving for a comfortable retirement.

Step 2: Determine Your Net Worth ?

What are you worth?

To determine how much you are worth, that is, your net worth, simply subtract your liabilities from your assets. This calculation will clearly show you your real wealth (or poverty, if you have been less than careful with your money in the past).

Assets

People can have some pretty strange ideas of what constitutes an asset because they usually confuse assets with things that have sentimental, or personal, value. Your favourite T-shirt of Elvis on figure skates is not an asset. So what is?

An asset is something you own that has value in the marketplace. There are two basic kinds of assets:

- personal use assets
- investment assets

Investment assets include cash, stocks, mutual funds, and bonds. We will discuss them in Chapter 7. Common types of personal use assets are:

- principal residence, summer residence (could also be an investment)
- sporting equipment
- appliances (this includes your personal, not business, computer, although its rate of depreciation means it won't be an asset for long)
- vehicles
- furniture
- camera equipment
- jewellery

Liabilities

When you purchase assets, it is important to remember the flip side: liabilities. This is the debt you incur to acquire your assets. Unless you have Bill Gates' wallet, you probably won't be able to pay for everything in cash. As you'll see, taking on debt to acquire assets is a normal practice that can work in your favour, as long as you do it sensibly.

Common liabilities:

- mortgages
- loans
- credit cards
- unpaid bills

Sample net worth form

If you have a computer, you can use one of the programs that are available to add up your assets and liabilities and figure out your net worth. Most of these programs are quite affordable and useful. Or you can just use this sample form and adjust it to fit your situation.

If you are in good financial health, you should have come out in the black. But you may not be as flush as you thought you were. You may want to figure out if you're making enough progress towards retirement. To figure out whether you have too many liabilities, look at your monthly payments for those liabilities. If they are more than 35 percent of your gross income, you may want to skip ahead to our discussion of debt management in Chapter 9. But before you have an anxiety attack, keep in mind that your net worth assessment does have a margin for error. For example, if you own a house, a drop in its market value could put you in the red, even though you're not planning to sell. Or a real estate bubble could make your net worth artificially high.

ASSETS

Deposit accounts
Institution

		amount
______		$ ______
______		$ ______
	total	$ ______

Life insurance (cash surrender value)
Company

		amount
______		$ ______
______		$ ______
	total	$ ______

Pensions and deferred profit-sharing plans
Company

		amount
______		$ ______
______		$ ______
	total	$ ______

Non-registered investments (stocks, funds, GICs, bonds, mortgages held, business interests, etc.)
Institution

		amount
______		$ ______
______		$ ______
	total	$ ______

RRSPs
Institution

		amount
______		$ ______
______		$ ______
	total	$ ______

Real estate (home, cottage, other)		amount
______		$ ______
______		$ ______
	total	$ ______

Other assets (equipment, furnishings, jewellery, art)		amount
______		$ ______
______		$ ______
	total	$ ______

Accounts receivable (loans made to family and friends, tax refunds owing)

		amount
______		$ ______
______		$ ______
	total	$ ______

TOTAL ASSETS $ ______

LIABILITIES

Mortgages

Lender ______________________ amount owing $ ______

Loans

1. Lender ______________________ amount owing $ ______

2. Lender ______________________ amount owing $ ______

Accounts payable
(credit cards, taxes, outstanding bills) ______

______

______

total $ ______

Other debt (guarantees, personal obligations) total $ ______

TOTAL LIABILITIES $ ______

NET WORTH

This is the big one. Subtract your total liabilities from your total assets. This is your net worth.

TOTAL ASSETS $ ______

TOTAL LIABILITIES – $ ______

TOTAL NET WORTH = $ ______

Goals for increasing your net worth

You've made a list of your retirement goals, and one way to make sure that they happen is to increase your net worth.

So now it's time to make a list of your goals for increasing your net worth before you retire. As you'll see, some of the things on the list will involve paying off debt, others will involve buying or selling assets, and maybe even incurring some more debt in the process. Your list might look something like this:

- I want to pay off my mortgage.
- I want to pay off my credit card debt.

- I want to buy a new home/vacation property/car.
- I want to increase my financial independence through investments.

These topics are all discussed in greater depth in the chapters to come.

APPRECIABLE VS DEPRECIABLE

When you are making a major purchase, such as buying a vacation property, a computer or a car, consider whether the asset is likely to appreciate or depreciate in value. If it is likely to depreciate, how long do you expect to own the asset? Do you expect to resell it? If so, will the difference in value be more than paid for by your use of the asset? Or are you better off renting? If it is likely to appreciate, how long can you expect to wait before you resell it? Would your money be better spent renting the object and putting the difference into a high-yield mutual fund?

Here are some ways to increase your net worth:

- Invest wisely. If you do this, your money should work harder and give you a better rate of return.
- When you get a raise, use the money to increase your savings or reduce your liabilities.
- Curb your spending habits.

Step 3: How Much You'll Need to Save

It's important to work out what you're going to need to live on in retirement, and although there's no magic formula, you should take three factors into consideration:

1) the number of years between now and retirement,
2) what you believe you'll need to live on per year, and
3) the effects of inflation.

Step 4: Calculate Your Current Income and Expenses

We suggest keeping an income and expense diary for at least two months. Subtract your expenses from your income. If you're in a good financial situation, this will give you a positive number. If you end up with a negative number, you're obviously spending more than you're making and you're in serious trouble. Or perhaps the two numbers are equal — in other words, you're spending everything that you're making and you're in a dangerous situation if hit with the loss of your job or unexpected expense. If you fall into either of these less desirable categories, don't despair. You can change your situation.

Step 5: Prepare a Budget

When you determined your income and your expenses, you may have discovered that your hard-earned money isn't going exactly where you want it to go. Maybe you're spending too much money on rent or your car expenses, or you're simply treating yourself to too many trips to Hawaii. So, now is the time to prepare a budget and actually direct your money in the way you want it to go. (Please see page 29 for sample budget form.) Look over your budget every so often to see if it is working for you, and change it as needed. Just keep your priorities in mind, and enjoy being in control of your financial life.

Notice that the monthly expenses section starts with a line for regular savings. That's where you would put the amount you've determined you'll need to set aside for retirement and other long-term goals.

The uncommitted income line at the bottom of the budget form is the amount of money you have left over, after you've met your day-to-day expenses and put aside the money you need for your long-term goals. You can use this however you want — in effect, it can be added to any expense line in the budget; so you might be cautious and save it, or you might use it for an expensive vacation.

BUDGET

Net monthly income		
Self (income after deductions, or take-home pay)		$ ______
Spouse (income after deductions, or take-home pay)		$ ______
Other income (pensions, investments, etc.)		$ ______
Total net income		$ ______
Monthly expenses		
Regular savings		$ ______
Payments on loans and debts		$ ______
Mortgage (principal and interest)		$ ______
Groceries		
– food	$ ______	
– cleaning supplies	$ ______	
– other	$ ______	$ ______
Clothing		$ ______
Shelter		
– rent	$ ______	
– repairs	$ ______	
– insurance	$ ______	
– taxes	$ ______	
– utilities	$ ______	$ ______
Transportation		
– gas	$ ______	
– repairs	$ ______	
– insurance	$ ______	
– parking	$ ______	
– other	$ ______	$ ______
Insurance premiums (direct medical/dental)		
– life	$ ______	
– disability	$ ______	
– health	$ ______	
– other	$ ______	$ ______
Recreation/Education		
– holidays	$ ______	
– hobbies	$ ______	
– clubs	$ ______	
– subscriptions	$ ______	$ ______
Income taxes		$ ______
Miscellaneous		
– donations	$ ______	
– dues	$ ______	
– childcare	$ ______	
– alimony	$ ______	
– child support	$ ______	
– other	$ ______	$ ______
Total expenses		$ ______
Uncommitted income (total net income less total expenses)		$ ______

Following Up

Once you've prepared a financial plan and put it into action, you have to follow it up in two ways:

- Monitor your progress. This means doing a net worth assessment at least annually by adding up your assets, subtracting your debts, and seeing if your net worth is growing every year. When you're young, you do an assessment primarily to establish the habit. Later on, the assessment tells you how you're doing and may raise an important warning flag — or give you good cause to pat yourself on the back.
- Every now and then, reassess your objectives. Sometimes a big event such as marriage, divorce, or receiving an inheritance makes the need to do so obvious. But you and your situation keep evolving over time, even without big events. Keep in touch with yourself.

Summary

With retirement no longer as far off as it once was, and you nearing the apex of your career, you should be socking away more money for your retirement than ever before. Start by calculating your personal worth (or that of your household), to determine where you are today. You should also be aware of which assets will appreciate between now and your retirement — your car won't be worth much, while your mutual funds and lakefront property probably will. But don't stop at that, set some goals to acquire other appreciating assets over the next few years to keep increasing your net worth before you retire.

QUICK RECAP

- **Determine your life goals.**
- **Calculate your net worth.**
- **Figure out how much you'll need to save for your goals.**
- **Calculate your current expenses using an expense diary.**
- **Prepare a budget that will meet your needs — both for today and for the future.**

CHAPTER 3

Retirement Countdown

Assess Your Situation

Now that you've accounted for your lifestyle goals, your net worth, your income, and your expenses, it's much easier to plan how you're going to get to your destination. And right now, your destination is retirement.

Your Retirement Age

First you'll need to know when you're likely to retire. Most pension plans, including CPP/QPP, specify age 65, and most Canadians still consider that the "normal" retirement age. If you go strictly by the government's RRSP book, your retirement age is 69. You can retire any time you can afford to. You cannot make contributions after the end of the year in which you turn 69, although you can still make spousal RRSP contributions if you have contribution room and if your spouse is under age 70. You can preserve your tax deferral by converting it into either a RRIF or an annuity.

How Much Does a Retired Person Need?

Although you may need $40,000 per year now, you'll likely not need quite as much when you retire. For one thing, you probably won't be contributing to your RRSP. You probably will have paid off your mortgage and sent your kids to school. There will usually be fewer big expenses left to pay off, but sometimes you need more than before in the early retirement years, to fund long-delayed goals like elaborate trips.

But remember that having enough to live on when you retire usually means more than just paying your own expenses. You may be trying to keep enough of an estate that it will benefit your heirs. Then again, you may never have married, and have one cat as a dependant. Whatever the future may hold for you, be optimistic about how much you're going to need. Better to have too much than too little. If you calculate your retirement needs at about 70 percent of your current income, adjusted for inflation, then you'll have a good ballpark figure for what you'll need.

The Fear of Falling Short

You may be thinking: At this rate, I'll only have 55 percent of my pre-retirement income to live on! What do I do? There are a couple of tactics. One is to take the advice in this book to heart and learn ways to maximize your retirement income. This might mean passing a little now on the extras to free up some cash for your hungry RRSP. Another tactic is to make retirement a time when you learn to live with less. But if you have a choice (and you do), it's wiser to enrich your future now rather than deal with the consequences later.

How Do You Save Enough? ?

No matter what you are saving for, you need to set up a separate savings account. You are less likely to touch savings if they are kept out of your expense accounts. Wherever you decide to put your savings, this place should have three main traits: it should be accessible, secure, and profitable. The most commonly used place for your funds is a savings account. The money is readily available, but interest rates are often quite low.

Money market mutual funds are a better short-term savings option. They often have higher returns than savings accounts. For long-term investing, money market mutual funds and savings accounts are not the place to be. You need a balanced portfolio of growth and income investments. Chapter 7 will go into types of investments in greater detail.

Reality Check

Now take a look at the following table. It shows you how many months it would take to save various amounts using monthly contributions to your RRSP. A common fear about retirement planning is that the saving won't be worth as much by the time you retire. However, you will be investing your savings so that you get a return that's higher than the inflation rate, so your purchasing power will grow.

NUMBER OF MONTHS IT WOULD TAKE TO SAVE

AMOUNT PER MONTH	$1,000	$2,500	$5,000	$7,500	$10,000
$50	19	44	77	104	127
$75	13	31	56	77	96
$100	10	24	44	61	77
$150	7	16	31	44	56
$200	5	12	24	35	44
$250	4	10	19	28	36
$500	2	5	10	15	19

Note: This table assumes a rate of return of 8 percent. The monthly contribution is invested at the beginning of the month, and interest is compounded monthly. No taxes or inflation are included in these calculations.

Adjusting for Inflation

If there were no inflation, you could simply multiply what you think you'll need to live on by the number of years you hope to live after retirement, and bingo, that would be what you'd need to save. The table on page 34 should give you some idea of how inflation forces you to earn more in order to keep your dollar's buying power.

IMPACT OF INFLATION ON PURCHASING POWER

Annual Rate of Inflation	Value Today	5 Years	10 Years	15 Years	20 Years	30 Years
3%	1,000	863	744	642	554	412
4%	1,000	822	676	555	456	308
5%	1,000	784	614	481	377	231
6%	1,000	747	558	417	312	174
7%	1,000	713	508	362	258	131
8%	1,000	681	463	315	215	99
9%	1,000	650	422	275	178	75
10%	1,000	621	386	239	149	57
11%	1,000	593	352	209	124	44
12%	1,000	567	322	183	104	33
13%	1,000	543	295	160	87	26

These projections are based on certain assumptions that are believed to be reasonable, but there is no assurance that the actual results will be consistent with this projection. The actual results may vary, perhaps to a material degree, from these projections.

Summary

After figuring out what sources of retirement income you will have, you need to assess how much you will need when you leave the workforce. Your financial needs depend on your retirement age, your expectations, and the spending habits that you identify in your expense diary. Your expenses probably won't be as high as they are now, because your mortgage should be paid off, and you probably aren't supporting your children to the degree you were 10 years ago. Once you've got an idea of how much income you'll need in your retirement, be aware of how long it takes to save the amount of money you need, and the negative role inflation plays. If you think that you'll need more income in your retirement than you expect to have, don't despair — you still have time to change your habits and invest wisely to make up the difference.

QUICK RECAP

1. **Determine how much annual income you will need in retirement.**
2. **Project whether your expected retirement resources will be sufficient to cover your retirement needs.**
3. **Determine the shortfall, if any.**
4. **Don't forget about inflation when making calculations for the future.**

CHAPTER 4

Cashing In on Retirement

Beth and John have spent many years dreaming about their retirement, but only in an abstract way. They have some vague plans to travel to exotic countries when they take early retirement, but they haven't thought much about where the money to fund their travels will come from. Beth and John haven't been maxing out their RRSPs in recent years because they have been saving to help send their four kids to university, and the cost of setting Beth's mother up in a good chronic care facility really took them by surprise. Fortunately, John has a pension plan, and the fact that they own a house in the city and a vacation home really puts them in good standing. If they can learn how to use their properties to their advantage, and start making their maximum RRSP contributions again, they'll be in great shape.

Sources of Retirement Income

Now that you have some idea of what retirement means to you and what assets you'll have to fund your lifestyle, the next step is to look at where that income might come from.

RRSPs and RRIFs

We'll go into much more detail on registered retirement savings plans (RRSPs) and registered retirement income funds (RRIFs) in Chapter 5, but for now what you need to know is that they're your best friend when it comes to providing for yourself in retirement. As of age 69, you're required to convert your RRSP to either a RRIF or a registered annuity. You must "mature" your RRSP no later than the end of the calendar year in which you turn 69, so you must select a retirement income program. This program could be a life annuity (with or without a guaranteed term), a term-certain annuity to age 90, or a RRIF, which has a required minimum payout. We talk a lot more about RRIFs in our book *Retire Ready*.

THE CONVERSION DEADLINE

If you miss the deadline for converting your RRSP into a RRIF or an annuity, the money in your RRSP will probably be fully taxable. MISSING THE DEADLINE COULD COST YOU UP TO HALF OF YOUR NEST-EGG with no avenue for appeal.

Annuities

Annuities are contracts that promise a future income stream provided by a financial institution (such as an insurance company, or a trust company) out of a lump sum you provide. Usually a monthly payment is made to you out of this fund. There are two main types of annuities: life annuities, which pay regularly for the rest of your life (generally available through insurance companies), and fixed-term annuities. There are all kinds of options available on annuity contracts, so consult a financial advisor concerning the fine print before you choose one.

Non-Registered Investments

Another source of income is, of course, any investments you hold outside of an RRSP. These might be stocks and bonds, real estate, or other assets that could provide you with an income.

Company Pension Plans

These are employer-sponsored pensions that are registered with Revenue Canada. Registered pension plans cover less than half of Canada's workforce and tend to be fairly heavily regulated. Your annual statement from your employer will project your annual pension based on current earnings, and will show how much you will have accumulated by the time you want to retire. Talk to your employer about when you will have access to your pension, and about whether you can take your pension with you if you decide to leave or are forced to leave the company.

Government Sources

CPP/QPP: The Canada and Quebec Pension Plans cover Canadians who work, either as employees or as self-employed individuals. Retirement benefits depend on your record of contributions and when you start taking benefits. You can start as early as age 60 or wait as late as age 70. For each month you claim before you turn 65, your payment is reduced by 0.5 percent (6 percent per year). For every month you wait after your 65th birthday, your payment increases by 0.5 percent. If you have a financial advisor, talk to him or her about whether you might benefit from starting the CPP/QPP early. (That way you can keep your RRSP tax-sheltered for longer.) You must apply for this benefit, so plan to contact Human Resources Development Canada or the Caisse de dépot et placement du Québec a few months before you retire.

TAKE ADVANTAGE OF THE CPP/QPP SPLIT

If one spouse is getting less CPP/QPP than the other, and you are in different tax brackets, you can plan to split each other's CPP/QPP benefits. That way you won't pay as much tax on the benefits.

Old Age Security (OAS)/Seniors' Benefit: Big changes are afoot. Starting in 2001, a new Seniors' Benefit will take effect for anyone aged 65 or older. The new Seniors' Benefit proposes to replace OAS, GIS, SPA, and the pension and age tax credits. Unlike the OAS, it would be tax-free, but the amount you would be entitled to will be based on a sliding scale measured against your income: the higher the income, the smaller the benefit.

The Empty Nest

There may soon come a time when you will want to downsize the family home. Older retirees find themselves, often enough, strained to maintain substantial homes. When they bought them, they could do most of the work themselves. People caught by the escalating demands (and costs) of aging dwellings often sell, though they would rather have spent their last years in familiar quarters. Others refuse to give up their homes, and become martyrs to them. Some are reluctant to part with valuable property they intend to pass along to their children, though the offspring may find themselves strapped for cash while the family wealth is locked up in real estate.

Once you are retired, your kids have left home and you have a couple of extra bedrooms, you may want to turn your empty nest into something that can help pay for your retirement. There are a few ways you can do this.

1. Sell the house, move into something smaller, and invest the leftover money in a retirement fund.
2. Take out a reverse mortgage on your house to supplement your income. A reverse mortgage means you can borrow money using your home as security for the loan. No payments or interest are due until you sell the house or reach the end of the mortgage term.
3. Alter your house so that it will provide income. But unless the place is already well-suited to such a purpose, that option could be less attractive than you might think. Costs could be very high, zoning restrictions may interfere, and in the end you will find that being a landlord or landlady is a part-time job you may not want.

Reverse Mortgages

As mentioned above, a reverse mortgage is a loan made out to you against a property you already own, debt-free. If you have property but little income, you can use it to beef up your income and finance anything you want. You don't have to pay the loan in the usual instalments; you just continue to own the home and live there (provided it is maintained and insured, and the taxes are paid). When the property is sold, or at the end of a stated term, the loan must be repaid with interest.

The financial institution gives you a line of credit or a lump sum. The total amount of the loan will usually not exceed 35 percent to 40 percent of the appraised value of the property. If you're so inclined, the loan proceeds can be used to buy an annuity, which in turn provides a regular income. Annuity interest is normally taxed, but in this case the mortgage becomes an investment loan, interest accruing offsets interest paid, and there's no income tax to pay. You can also use a reverse mortgage to pass along some or all of the cash to your children, perhaps to help them buy places of their own, taking the sting out of the encumbrance the property carries when you pass it along to the next generation. You can also tailor the deal so that a minimum portion of the value of the home will go to your estate, even if it's worth less than the amount of the mortgage and its accrued interest.

What if the mortgage ends up worth more than the property? The lender has no recourse if the value of the property drops below the total accrued principal and interest on the mortgage.

Where's the catch?

None of this is as attractive to a lender as a mortgage in the usual form, so don't expect to get the interest rate or the loan amount you could receive if you were a new purchaser — at least, not right after retirement. The older you are, the sooner the mortgage company can expect to see its money back; hence, the better the deal they can offer you. Before you sign up for a reverse mortgage, take the time to get some legal advice and consider it carefully.

Summary

As you know by now, retirement living means doing what you dream of. If you plan, save, and prepare for your future, you'll be able to retire in style. There are various sources of income that you can draw on during your retirement: private investments, a company pension plan, and government funds. One of the real tricks to funding your retirement is knowing in what order to cash in your investments. Because these incomes will come to you in different amounts at different times, it is important to determine how much income you will receive from each source, and how often, during your retirement. You'll need expert advice on how to time the sale of your investments to minimize the taxes due.

QUICK RECAP

1. **Make sure you have multiple sources of retirement income, and make sure you know how much will be coming to you.**
2. **Be sure to consider:**
   - **RRSPs**
   - **RRIFs**
   - **government sources**
   - **annuities**
   - **company pension plans**
   - **other investments**

CHAPTER 5

From Here to Retirement

The Little Savings Plan That Grew

Unless you live where there are no televisions or magazines, you probably know that the initials RRSP stand for registered retirement savings plan. Every RRSP is registered with Revenue Canada as an authorized savings plan. Building an RRSP is one of the only ways you can shelter your money for the future without losing much of it to taxes. It should be the cornerstone of healthy retirement planning. Each year, the government will allow you to invest money in an RRSP designed to provide you with retirement income. The amount is reduced if you are a member of a registered pension plan. Not only do you pay no tax on the money in your RRSP as it's growing, but your yearly contribution is also tax deductible. So there is incentive to invest as much as you can, which will grow over time into a healthy nest egg. Don't overdo it — there are penalties for overcontributing to your RRSP.

Where Can You Buy One?

Before you sign up for an RRSP, do a little bit of comparison shopping. Banks aren't the only places you can buy an RRSP — most financial institutions offer them, including trust companies, credit unions, life insurance companies, investment dealers, and mutual fund companies. You will find that investment dealers and mutual fund companies offer as wide a range of RRSP options as the banks do. Wherever your RRSP is currently registered, you may want to ensure you are informed about your alternatives.

Minimize Your Taxes

Putting part of your income towards an RRSP isn't the only way to reduce your tax bill. Here are a few more ways you can make your money go further.

Transfer tax free

If you receive a lump sum retiring allowance or a severance package, you may be able to transfer part or all of it to your RRSP on a tax-deferred basis, which means it will be taxable when it is withdrawn from your RRSP.

Create a spousal RRSP

If you make more money than your spouse, it may make sense to set up and contribute to a spousal RRSP. It is owned by your spouse, but you receive the tax deduction for the contribution. If your spouse will be in a lower tax bracket when the money is withdrawn in retirement, the income withdrawn from it will be taxed at a lower rate. It also establishes a source of retirement income that can qualify for the pension income credit in the spouse's hands after age 65. Note that if a spousal RRSP is redeemed too soon after the last contribution to any spousal RRSP, the person who got the tax benefit from the contribution may be required to include the redeemed amount in their income. Consult a financial advisor to avoid this costly error.

Putting your pension in your RRSP

If you are one of the lucky ones who participates in a registered pension plan with your employer, and you leave that job, you might consider transferring your vested pension funds into an RRSP. Vested benefits are locked in, which means that they can't be paid back as a cash refund. They can sometimes be transferred to a locked-in RRSP. This type of RRSP has restrictions on the maximum amount that can be withdrawn annually. Some provinces have restrictions on the age at which withdrawals can begin. These restrictions ensure that the money is used for retirement income.

Should You Borrow to Buy Your RRSP?

It is a good idea to contribute the maximum amount to your RRSP each year. In February, you should max out your contribution if you haven't already done so. It can be a good strategy to borrow to make your contribution if you don't have enough cash. The interest on the money you borrow isn't tax deductible, but the cost of borrowing may still be outweighed by the increase in value of your RRSP as well as the value of your tax deduction. Many financial institutions offer good rates for RRSP loans, if you get the RRSP with their company. It is even possible to find a company that will defer repayment of the loan for up to 120 days, enough time to convert your tax refund into a loan payment.

Becoming Your Own RRSP Manager

You probably know that RRSPs are administered through financial institutions, but did you know that you can manage your own RRSP portfolio? A self-directed RRSP involves more work than having a manager look out for your money, and you are entirely responsible for doing your own research and monitoring investments outside of any mutual fund investments. But for some people, they offer a great feeling of accomplishment.

Moreover, there are some types of investments that are open only to self-directed RRSP holders. Be warned though: you have to know what you are doing and what types of investments are available to you, as well as keep abreast of changes that the government makes to RRSP rules. There is no investment advisor or money manager to hold your hand with these plans, so your risk is greater.

Self-directed plans generally have fees attached, usually $100 to $150 per plan every year.

The Last Word on RRSPs

They're the best way to shelter your money and defer taxes. Even if you put only tiny amounts into it, you'll be doing yourself more good than if you never bother. There is no down side to RRSPs — they help you now and they help you later.

Investing $500 a Month Inside and Outside an RRSP

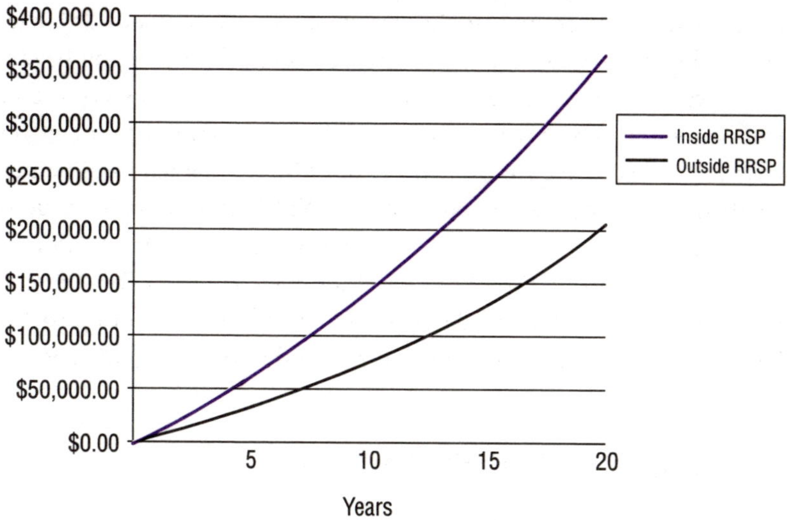

Note: This graph assumes a rate of return of 8 percent. The monthly contribution is invested at the beginning of the month, and interest is compounded monthly. The inflation rate is 3 percent, and the taxation rate is 28 percent.

TALK TO THE EXPERTS

Take advantage of the legions of experts who can advise you about setting up an RRSP, selecting the right mix of investments, and reviewing it on a regular basis.

Take My Money, Please

The easiest way to stick to your contribution plan is to arrange with your financial institution for a pre-authorized automatic investment plan to debit your account each month. Now you don't have to think about making the investments yourself, and you take advantage of your RRSP contributions working for you earlier in the year.

If your RRSP is invested in a mutual fund, there's another good reason to make regular monthly investments rather than one annual contribution. Making regular investments takes advantage of price fluctuations within your funds. At the end of each year, not only will you have compounded your rate of return on 12 separate investments, but you'll have purchased your funds for a price averaged out over the year. (This is called dollar-cost averaging. It is discussed in more detail in Chapter 6.)

PAY YOURSELF FIRST

Allotting part of your budget for investing is an important first step to reaching your retirement goals. Decide how much you want to invest and then put a set amount from each paycheque towards your investments. How much you put aside each month is, of course, up to you, and will vary depending on your income and your financial responsibilities.

Gord and Shelly had been putting $300 a month into their RRSPs, which they thought was pretty good. But when they looked at the 10 percent rule (save 10 percent of your income each month), they realized they should be investing double that. If you already have an automatic investment plan, is it time to increase the amount you put in? Are you earning more than you were when you set up the savings plan? Do you have fewer responsibilities? Could you be putting more into your RRSP?

Financial Habits

Cutting expenses is only the most obvious way of squeezing savings out of your budget. Take a look at the following lists of habits you can either develop or squelch to make the most of your income. Many of these ideas are further explained in later chapters.

HABITS THAT HURT

- ✗ Buying things you don't really need.
- ✗ Keeping your money in a low-interest account and letting inflation eat away at it.
- ✗ Missing the RRSP deadline because you don't have the cash for a lump sum payment. This also means you won't get a tax deduction and you'll pay more tax than you need to. Write reminders on your calendar or in your planner to make saving for the deadline a priority (or better yet, contribute monthly).
- ✗ Signing up for more credit cards than necessary. Just because a company sends you an application for a gold card doesn't mean you have to bite. Getting closer to retirement, enticements to get into debt are temptations to be avoided.

HABITS THAT HELP

- ✔ Working out a budget for the year, and sticking to it. (Be sure to build in a contingency fund to cover unexpected bills — your car blows a gasket, you or a family member are injured and need to take time off work.)
- ✔ Paying yourself first by starting, or increasing, your automatic investment plan. See your financial institution about having a percentage of your paycheque automatically moved to your RRSP account. At this phase of your life, it's probably a good idea to max out on the RRSP.
- ✔ Planning for your needs once you retire. You're going to have new activities, and probably some new spending habits, too. Looking ahead to prepare for these changes is an excellent strategy.
- ✔ Assessing how you use your credit cards. Are you able to pay them off each month? Are you at risk of having to use your RRSP income to pay off your cards once you retire? If so, perhaps you should consider using your debit card instead. (Credit cards usually cost a whopping 16 to 18 percent interest a month; department store cards cost 25 to 30 percent a year.) For more on the proper use of credit and debit cards, see Chapter 9.
- ✔ Becoming a smart consumer. Research major purchases before buying. Check consumer magazines for repair records and ratings of cars and appliances. Shop around for the best deal (this goes for things like auto insurance, too).
- ✔ Looking into borrowing if you can't max out your RRSP this year. Often, the cost of borrowing is more than outweighed by the increase in value in your RRSP as well as the value of your tax deduction from the RRSP contribution.

Summary: The Seven Magic Words

Here's a tidy summary of this chapter, reduced to a list of seven words you could easily stick on your fridge. These are the cornerstones of making your retirement nest egg grow.

Choose: Set retirement and tax planning goals both for your distant future and your near future.

Plan: Work towards your goals by calculating how much you need to save.

Discipline: Learn to save with regularity. You won't fritter away small amounts now that could add up to big amounts later.

Authorize: Start an automatic payment plan direct to your RRSP.

Maximize: Take advantage of price fluctuations and compound rates of return by making monthly investments into your RRSP.

Listen: Be aware of changes to RRSP legislation, especially if you have a self-directed RRSP.

Live: Try to strike a balance between being diligent and being obsessed. By being happy rather than stressed, you'll have a better chance of being around when it comes time to enjoy all that money you've saved.

QUICK RECAP

1. **Check out the alternatives for RRSPs — find the best place to buy yours.**
2. **Look into ways to minimize your taxes in conjunction with your RRSP.**
3. **Take advantage of professional services, such as dealing with a financial advisor and having funds automatically deposited into your RRSP every month.**
4. **Work on improving your good financial habits and taming the bad ones.**

CHAPTER 6

Investing in High Gear

Maggie, the graphic designer, has never done much investing — she thought that was only for risk takers and high-rollers and that she'd be better off keeping the savings for her and her daughter in a simple savings account. But now that she is saving more for her retirement, identifying her retirement goals and her uncommitted income, Maggie wants to find ways to make her money grow faster. Because she only knows the basics about investing, she decided to find a financial advisor who would help her determine what kinds of investments are right for her and answer any questions she might have about these investments. Once she has settled on a suitable investment portfolio, Maggie will be able to sit back and watch her returns come rolling in much faster than they would have in her old savings account.

Even a loonie in a piggybank loses value to inflation. But smart investing allows you to beat inflation by making that loonie worth more, rather than less. Investing your money in the right place can give you financial security, increase your net worth, and take you many steps toward financial independence. You can set a sound investment strategy by understanding the characteristics of different types of investments and creating the right balanced mix that helps your money grow and lets you sleep at night. Your best way of developing that strategy is doing it with the help of a professional financial advisor.

Selecting a Financial Advisor

Financial advisors take the time to know the lifestyle and financial needs of their clients. They have invested their time and energy into becoming knowledgeable in investments, taxation, estate planning, insurance, and retirement planning. In addition, they may work with a network of specialists who can provide the in-depth knowledge needed to deal with situations as they arise.

Search for a financial advisor who combines an understanding of people with knowledge of technical planning matters. Most will provide you with an opportunity to learn about the processes they use and will give detailed information on the services they offer and the company they work for before expecting you to begin the financial planning process. Things to look for in choosing an advisor:

- You feel compatible with the advisor and feel you can work well together.
- The advisor has an appropriate educational background.
- The advisor belongs to a professional association that has a code of ethics and standards.
- The advisor works for an established, solid financial institution.
- The advisor is willing to explain how he or she comes to a complete understanding of your current and desired personal, family, and financial situation.
- The same advisor who meets with you initially will continue to work on all of your subsequent needs.
- The advisor will review your situation at least annually.
- The advisor fully reveals how he or she is compensated for working on your account.

Know Yourself

When you start setting up your portfolio, you'll have to do some soul searching to match your investment mix to your goals and time frame. Ask yourself first about your time horizon and risk tolerance. What is the worst-case scenario? Remember, it is always a good idea to have a professional advisor help you through this process. Take stock of who and where you are, where you want to go, and how long you have to get there. Find out what sort of risk you are comfortable with.

- **Attitude**: Are you the kind of person who lies awake worrying about whether your financial institution will be struck by lightning? If so, you probably won't tolerate a lot of risk in your investment portfolio, and you'd be better off investing your money conservatively.
- **Age**: How old are you? If you're young and have few responsibilities, you can afford to take greater risks with investments for your long-term goals and you have more time to ride out any market lows your investments encounter. Once you get older and closer to retirement, you'll want to shift some of your investments into a more conservative portfolio.
- **Responsibilities**: Who or what depends on your income? If you have dependants, a mortgage, or a substantial loan to support, you probably can't afford to take great risk, so you'll want to invest most of your money conservatively.
- **Cash flow**: What's your income like? Is your job steady? If your cash flow is erratic or likely to decrease, you don't want to risk investing in something that is too volatile.
- **Net worth**: If you have a large cushion to soften the blow of any losses, a long timeline, and a growing tolerance for risk, you can afford to accept more volatility.
- **Time horizon**: The longer you expect to keep your money in an investment, the greater the volatility you can manage because over time, short-term drops in the value of an investment should be replaced by gains.
- **Desired rate of return**: Different assets have different risk levels and therefore different potential rates of return.

Assessing Your Risk Tolerance

Only you know your attitude toward risk, so you must assess your own comfort zone. Ask yourself, "What's the worst that can happen if this doesn't work?" If "the worst" is something you can live with, then the risk is acceptable. Keep in mind that there is risk in not investing or in investing where, after tax, returns are less than inflation. The risk is that your purchasing power will decrease. Smart investing means having the appropriate balance of different investments to provide long-term growth with a risk level that is acceptable to you. The longer you have until you need the money, the more you can use investments with higher variability. This is because historically markets have tended to climb over time while experiencing peaks and valleys. The mix and balance of your investment portfolio will evolve as you get closer to the time you need the money.

In determining what risk is acceptable to you, keep in mind your short- and long-term goals. If you are planning to buy a second home next year, you don't want to put your down-payment money into the stock market now, no matter how high it's soaring. A market downturn that coincides with your purchase date would have a serious impact on your short-term goal.

Although assessing your risk tolerance is largely a personal matter, some principles apply to just about everyone. For example, a 40-year-old can tolerate more investment risk than a 60-year-old who is looking to retire in the next few years. The closer you are to needing your nest egg, the less you're going to want to have in more volatile investments. One very rough way of calculating this "age/risk ratio" is to subtract your age from 100. The number left over will be the percentage that you can afford to put in higher-return, higher-risk investments, such as equities. So if you're 45 years old, 55 percent of your investment portfolio might be in equities. As you get older, this percentage will shrink. An advisor can help you make the right decision on your investment portfolio mix.

WHAT'S YOUR TOLERANCE?

Risk means different things to different people. Here is a relative yardstick for investment risk that can help you decide where your emotional comfort level is.

None: Your only concern is for the security of your original principal and you aren't interested in retaining its purchasing power over time.

Low: You could tolerate a fluctuation of no more than 10 percent in the value of your investment, occurring rarely, and even this would make you uneasy.

Moderate: You would not panic over a fluctuation of 10 to 20 percent in the value of your investment at any given time, knowing that over the long term you would eventually benefit from a positive return.

High: You could handle a fluctuation of 20 to 50 percent in the value of your investment at any given time in return for the potential for longer-term growth.

Very High: You could tolerate 50 percent or more in the value of your investment, as long as you'd see a large potential return in the future.

Managing Risk

You can't and shouldn't avoid risk, but you can manage it. It is rather like driving a car on a highway. There's always some risk of accident or injury, but you can "manage" the risk by wearing a seatbelt, driving at a sensible speed, ensuring that the car is well maintained, and so on. You can reduce the risk even further by not making the trip, or by never leaving your home. But in reducing the risk of a highway accident by never leaving your home, you increase the risk of perpetual unemployment. Similarly, you can reduce the risk of investment losses to near zero by keeping your money under your mattress, but that increases the risk of losing purchasing power to inflation.

You shouldn't fret about investment risk. Higher-risk investments generally have the potential for a higher return. The key is to understand the risks and, with the help of a professional advisor, build a portfolio that has the right level and mix of risks. You should, however, be aware of the different kinds of risk and how they affect different investments.

Inflation risk: This is a special concern for GICs and other so-called risk-free investments. If, for example, inflation is 3 percent, a GIC at 5 percent over five years will give a real return of only 2 percent, and you likely will have lost purchasing power after tax. Unless they are held in an RRSP, you must also pay tax on GIC interest annually.

Interest rate risk: As interest rates rise, the market value of bonds falls. This is a concern if you have to sell a bond before it matures.

Currency risk: Fluctuating exchange rates can cut into your return on investments made in foreign markets.

Economic risk: Certain industries are very sensitive to fluctuations in the economy. The auto industry tends to do well in good times. Others, including utilities such as electrical power and telecommunications, are less sensitive to economic cycles.

Industry risk: With the rapid pace of technological change, some industries such as the computer industry, are inherently volatile.

Company risk: When you own a stock, you own part of a business, and even businesses in booming industries can be poorly managed.

Credit risk: If you're buying bonds, you're lending money to a company or government. Interest payments could be suspended or you may not be repaid your principal if the borrower runs into financial difficulty.

Liquidity risk: How easy is it to get your money with minimal capital loss? An account at a financial institution is liquid. Real estate is less liquid because you can't sell it until you find a buyer.

Political risk: Governments change the rules.

Evaluating the Performance of Your Investments

The press have a lot to say about the performance of investments, particularly mutual funds. Sensational headlines with this week's tragedies and tomorrow's predictions abound. When evaluating your investments — either over your morning newspaper and coffee, or formally with your financial advisor — be sure to follow these three simple rules:

Compare apples to apples. A mutual fund containing Pacific Rim stocks is much more volatile than one containing mortgages. They are different asset classes, with different risks and serving different purposes in your investment plan. As you can see from the table on the next page, the best and worst one-year periods for these investments vary widely.

There are no crystal balls. No one could have predicted what day you should have invested in order to have "ridden the wave" to the one-year 129.5% return on Japanese stocks. If that sort of prediction were possible, everyone would also have avoided the single-year loss of −42.1% in the same market! Your best bet is to be in a mix of asset classes, all of the time. That's why mutual funds make such excellent sense for most investors and why it's so important to include foreign content in your long-term RRSP.

Time reduces risk. The one-year highs and lows in the table demonstrate the relative volatility of each asset class. The average five-year returns demonstrate how time invested in a particular market or asset class reduced that level of volatility. Be patient if you can.

Developing an Investment Strategy

A sound investment strategy starts with a good understanding of your financial goals. One approach is to divide your assets into three "pots" — to meet short-, mid- and long-term goals. An example of a long-term goal is to create an investment portfolio that will provide you with the

CASH & CASH EQUIVALENTS	HIGHEST 1-YEAR RETURN	LOWEST 1-YEAR RETURN	AVERAGE 5-YEAR ANNUAL RETURN
Savings Accounts	11.6%	0.5%	5.3%
90-day deposits	14.0%	4.5%	9.1%
Canada Savings Bonds	19.1%	5.1%	9.4%
5-year GICs	14.8%	5.8%	10.0%

FIXED INCOME INVESTMENTS	HIGHEST 1-YEAR RETURN	LOWEST 1-YEAR RETURN	AVERAGE 5-YEAR ANNUAL RETURN
Mortgages	34.8%	−2.0%	11.7%
Bonds	55.6%	−10.4%	13.7%
Dividend Stocks	79.5%	−14.5%	12.5%
Real Estate	19.3%	−7.1%	7.5%

EQUITY INVESTMENTS	HIGHEST 1-YEAR RETURN	LOWEST 1-YEAR RETURN	AVERAGE 5-YEAR ANNUAL RETURN
Canadian Index	86.9%	−18.5%	9.7%
U.S. Index	56.9%	−22.8%	15.7%
Japanese Index	129.5%	−42.1%	15.6%
World Index	63.5%	−23.2%	13.0%
European Index	111.5%	−23.5%	17.1%

INFLATION	HIGHEST 1-YEAR RATE	LOWEST 1-YEAR RATE	AVERAGE 5-YEAR ANNUAL RATE
Consumer Price Index	8.3%	−0.2%	3.7%

Notes: This table contains historical data and there is no assurance that future results will be consistent with this table. All rates of return occurred during the period January 1, 1982 to December 31, 1996.

funds you need to retire comfortably in 15 years. A mid-term goal is to replace your car in five years. A short-term goal is to fund the down payment on a vacation property next summer. Assume only as much risk as you need to meet each goal.

Money from each "pot" can be distributed among three classes of investments: cash or cash equivalents, meaning liquid investments, such as government savings bonds, T-bills, and money market funds; fixed-income securities, which pay a fixed income and are held for a term of over a year, such as GICs, and fixed-income mutual funds; and equity investments, which can potentially provide the highest gains, but which also come with the greatest volatility, including Canadian and international stocks, and equity mutual funds. Think of your portfolio as being made up of both your RRSPs and your other investments, which are probably not tax-sheltered. In your short-term pot, you will want to have most of your investments in fixed income and cash equivalents. In your long-term pot, you should include more variable investments, such as Canadian and foreign equities, to achieve bigger rewards. The medium-term pot will contain a balance of the two.

Asset Allocation

To tailor your portfolio to your own investment needs, ask yourself the following:

- How much do I need to keep available for emergencies and short-term goals?
- How much do I need to invest for the long term?
- Will I benefit more from a compounding rate of return or do I need income from my investments?
- What are the tax consequences of my investment?
- How much variability am I willing to accept?

Your investment strategy should consist of dividing your assets in such a way that your investments are diversified. This strategy is called asset allocation. The strategy involves building a portfolio that includes assets from each of the three asset categories (cash, fixed income, and equity), in the Canadian market as well as international markets. How much you invest in each category is determined by your tolerance for risk and your time horizon. Peaks in the performance of one category will tend to balance out valleys in another and the overall result should be closer to steady growth than you would achieve by putting all your eggs in one basket. Most financial professionals agree that asset allocation — the correct proportion of stocks, bonds and cash — is more important to total portfolio performance than picking the top performers.

If you suddenly wake up in a cold sweat on your fiftieth birthday and you realize that you haven't saved enough to maintain your lifestyle in retirement, don't panic and throw all your money into high-return, high-risk investments in the hope of making up for lost time. Without setting out a good strategy, you could end up losing more than you make. Make achieving a balance between risk and reward your highest priority, and you'll make the most of what you have.

CHOOSING A FINANCIAL INSTITUTION

Different institutions offer different products, services, fees, advice levels, and options, so it's important to find one that's right for your needs. After all, you're trusting them not just with your money, but with your future, as well. So make sure you choose a financial institution that you feel comfortable dealing with and that offers services suited to your needs.

INVESTMENT VEHICLES RATED BY RISK, RETURN, AND REQUIRED KNOWLEDGE

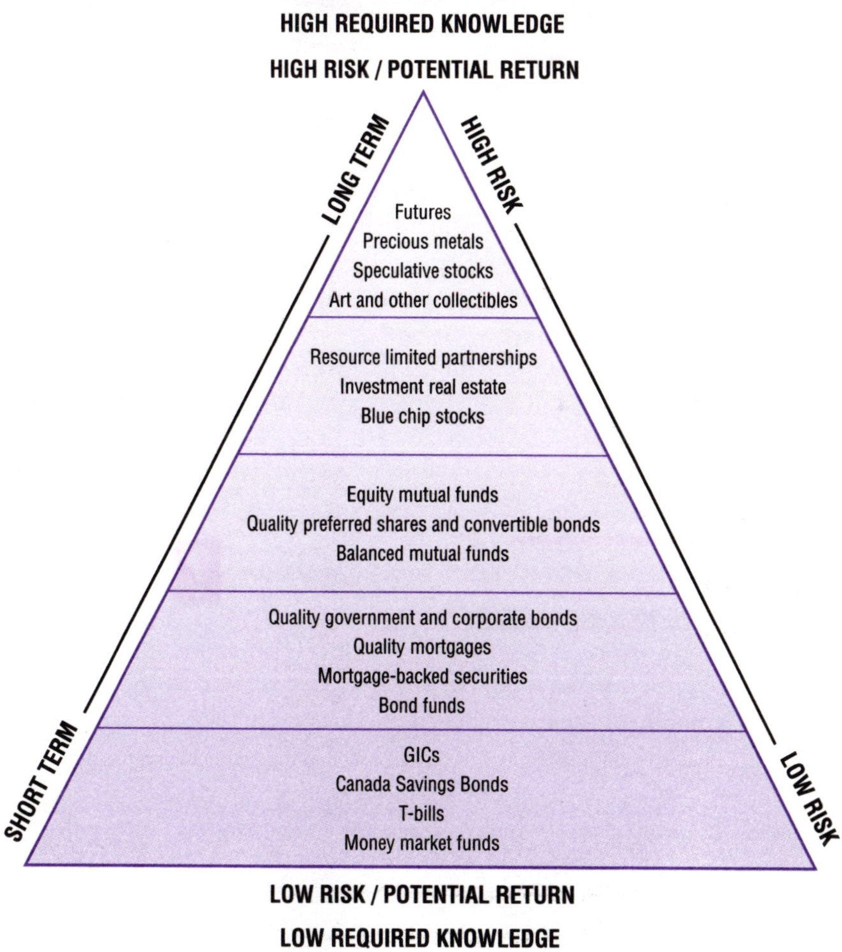

As Markets Move – Stay the Course

Once you've developed your asset mix, review it at least annually and rebalance to maintain your desired asset mix. Remember you are looking for long-term growth, so don't vary your asset mix with every move in the markets. An asset mix is also relatively easy to align with your age/risk ratio. With retirement approaching, you can adjust your mix toward fixed-income securities and cash, maintaining a smaller percentage in growth investments. Remember age may not be the most critical factor. The key is time, not timing. Don't tinker too often and use an investment professional to help you build the right mix of investments.

Dollar-Cost Averaging

Dollar-cost averaging is a technique that involves buying equal dollar amounts of a given investment on a regular basis, such as $100 every month. It works well for investments that fluctuate in price, such as shares and mutual funds. In fact, it lets you take advantage of those fluctuations. By buying a fixed dollar amount of an investment every month, you buy more units of the security when the price is low, and fewer units when the price is high. If the investment tends to rise in price over time, the end result is a reduction of the average price paid for the investment purchased. (See the charts on pages 59–60.)

Should You Pay Down Your Mortgage or Contribute to Your RRSP?

This is a question that a lot of homeowners ask because they often view both paying down their mortgage and building their RRSP as top priorities. The answer varies from person to person, and depends on factors such as your age and retirement plans. But ideally you should be able to do both. If you maximize your RRSP contribution, you can put your tax refund toward paying down your mortgage. Or, consider maximizing your RRSP this year and make a large mortgage payment next year. Don't forget that any unused RRSP contribution room can be carried forward to the next year.

THE EVER-INCREASING PATTERN

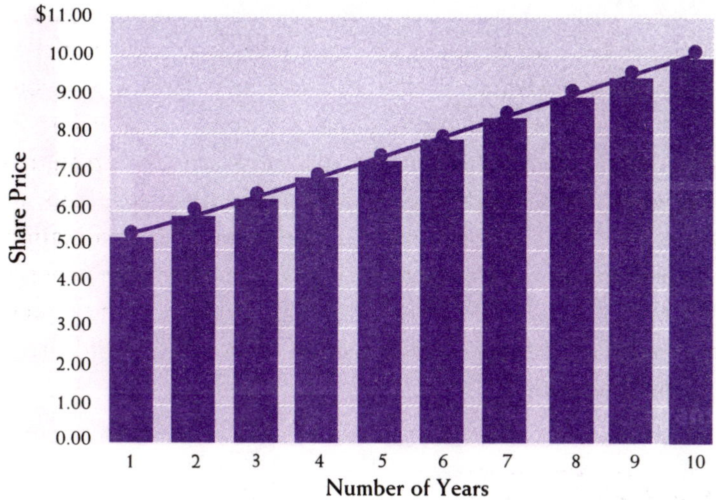

Original unit price	$5.00	Final unit price	$10.00
Total units purchased	1,699	Average price paid	$7.19
Total value of units	$16,686.00	Gain on investment	$4,686.00

THE DOWN-AND-UP PATTERN

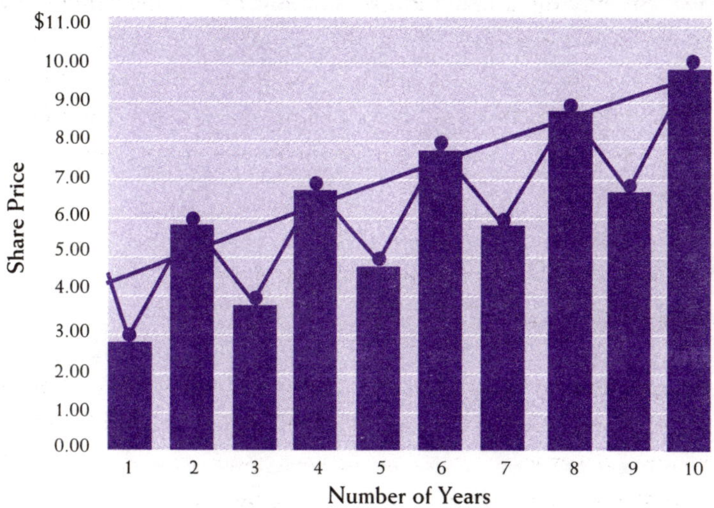

Original unit price	$5.00	Final unit price	$10.00
Total units purchased	2,075	Average price paid	$5.78
Total value of units	$20,746.00	Gain on investment	$8,746.00

THE DECLINE-AND-RETURN-TO-ORIGINAL-PRICE PATTERN

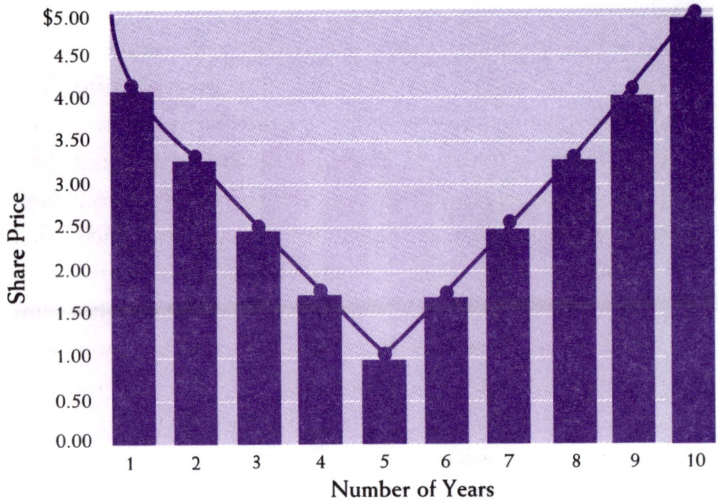

Original unit price	$5.00	Final unit price	$5.00
Total units purchased	4,829	Average price paid	$2.48
Total value of units	$24,147.00	Gain on investment	$12,147.00

Diversify Your Holdings

A successful asset mix depends not on being in the right market at the right time, but on being in most markets all of the time, with varying exposures. If you've created an asset mix for your investments, you've already diversified your holdings to a degree. Diversification, however, doesn't just mean putting money into different investment vehicles. If you own a home, you have a substantial investment in your local community. If you're in a one-industry town, you work in that industry and have purchased stock in the company you work for, your assets are very concentrated. Look into investments that will move some of your assets out of your community, out of your industry and even out of Canada — our economy can take a downturn while others are on the rise. International mutual funds now make these investments feasible, even if you're not among the jet set.

Summary

Your investment portfolio is a personal thing, and should reflect you and your needs. The type of investments you should get into depends on factors such as your age, attitude, responsibilities, and when you want to retire. Working with a financial advisor is one way to feel secure about your investments. An advisor will help you learn about yourself by assessing what kind of investments are right for you, and will show you how to build a diversified investment portfolio that suits your needs. To get more out of your investments, use dollar-cost averaging and invest a fixed sum in your retirement portfolio every month. If you have planned your portfolio properly, and feel confident in your choice of financial advisor, you should be able resist shuffling your investments around when periodic market scares strike. You and your professional advisor should review your portfolio at least once a year, but other than that, just sit tight and watch it grow.

QUICK RECAP

1. **Find a professional financial advisor with whom you feel comfortable.**
2. **Build your portfolio around your goals, risk tolerance, and time horizon, but remember that you can't avoid risk altogether.**
3. **Make sure that your total portfolio contains a mix of cash, fixed-income securities, and equity investments.**
4. **Review your portfolio at least annually, but don't react to every blip in the market — you are investing for the long term.**

CHAPTER 7

Investment Vehicles

Types of Investments

In order to be an informed investor, you should understand what you're buying, what the investment is intended to do, and what the risks and tax consequences of your investment are. Let's get started by looking at the two basic categories of investments: debt and equity.

Debt investments

Governments, corporations, individuals, and other entities borrow money for a variety of purposes. These loans are called bonds. If you invest in one of these, you are the lender. You want to know:

- your prospects for getting your money back,
- what income you can expect while you hold the investment, and
- when and how you will receive both.

Debt instruments pay you interest. Once a bond is issued, it gains in value if interest rates drop, and vice versa; therefore it may also provide capital gains or losses, which receive different tax treatment than interest.

Equity investments

These are usually shares in a company. They represent part ownership in the venture, with the prospect of all its risks and rewards. You need to know something about the company, its prospects, its market, and its competitors before you buy its shares. Equities offer the potential for capital gains and may pay dividends.

Variations on the basics

There is a wide variety of investment products. The best-known and easiest to understand are mutual funds. But whatever investment you choose, there is always more to know about it than first appears. It's essential to stay informed and up to date. Choose your advisors well.

Time and Timing

You can invest your money for periods ranging from less than 30 days to more than 30 years. Long-term debt instruments imply a forecast of inflation and interest rates for decades ahead — obviously something of a risk. If you're right, the rewards can be high. Some people still hold double-digit government bonds they bought when inflation was high. With stocks, the tendencies are reversed. They can be flipped in minutes, but that requires close attention and sometimes approaches gambling. Longer-term equity holdings are most consistently profitable. In general, short-term investing involves short-term management, which takes up more of your time — but any investment must be watched. It all boils down to when you buy the investment, how long you hold it, and when you sell it.

Value

When you're buying, selling, or trading investments, remember that the "value" of something — especially share equity — is not necessarily what you think it should be. It's no more than a buyer is willing to pay for it.

Looking into the Alternatives

What follows is a quick guide to the most common types of investments out there. They include debt and equity investments, and they have varying degrees of risk and reward. Read through these options and then talk them over with your financial advisor to decide which investments are right for you.

Types of Debt Investments

Interest or fixed-income investments

When you buy a fixed-income investment, your income is defined at the outset. It could be fixed or have different rates for different periods. You may receive your income when the term is up, or periodically over time. The same applies to your principal (if you invest in an amortized mortgage, for instance, with each payment you get some of your money back). If your risk tolerance is low, you'll want the majority of your investments in these vehicles. But don't expect to make your fortune this way. To calculate your real earnings, subtract taxes, then the rate of inflation. For example, suppose:

- your rate of return is 8 percent,
- you're in a 50 percent tax bracket, and
- inflation is 3 percent.

Your real rate of return is only 1 percent (8 – 4 – 3 = 1). Your tax rate will be determined by your income bracket. Assuming your borrower is reliable, your two greatest risks in a fixed-income investment are that inflation will wipe out your earnings (suppose, in the example, that inflation hits 5 percent or 6 percent), or that you'll be locked into a fixed return when current interest rates rise.

Canada Savings Bonds (CSBs)

- these are specific government bonds that cannot be traded, only kept or cashed in
- pay interest (after the first three months) to the end of the previous month
- interest income is fully taxable each year when held outside of an RRSP
- a safe and easy investment
- available at most financial institutions

- set at a fixed interest rate (which may change over the course of the term)
- easy to cash (high liquidity)
- available for as little as $100

Treasury bills (T-bills)

- these government-issued investments pay a specified return for a specified (usually short) period
- interest income is fully taxable each year when held outside of an RRSP
- safe; considered equivalent to cash
- issued by the Government of Canada and provincial governments for terms of 91, 182, and 364 days
- can be bought and sold at any time from banks and brokers
- defined rate of return
- usually sold in amounts from $5,000 to $25,000 or higher
- bought at a discount and mature at face value

Term deposits

- vehicles for depositing a fixed sum of money for a fixed period of time at a fixed or variable interest rate
- offered by most financial institutions
- usually carry a guaranteed rate of interest for the length of the term
- interest income is fully taxable each year when held outside of an RRSP
- not meant to be redeemed, so if redeemed, may be subject to penalties
- $500 minimum, usually invested for periods ranging from 30 to 364 days
- may be covered by federal deposit insurance (CDIC)
- a term deposit of less than one year is called a certificate of deposit; anything longer is a GIC

Guaranteed investment certificates (GICs)

- interest-bearing deposits where interest can be paid periodically or upon maturity
- safe: covered by CDIC for up to $60,000 if purchased from an institution belonging to CDIC and the term is five years or less (If you have more than $60,000 to invest, buy from more than one insured institution.)

CDIC DEPOSIT INSURANCE

The Canada Deposit Insurance Corporation (CDIC) is a federal government agency that insures eligible deposits at member institutions. These include most banks and trust companies in Canada, but check if you're not sure whether a particular institution qualifies. If it does, your eligible deposits are automatically insured. "Eligible" means, generally, savings, GICs, chequing, and term deposits in Canadian dollars. GICs must be repayable within five years. The maximum amount the CDIC will protect in one name at one institution is $60,000 in principal and interest in all your deposits and accounts. If you have more to invest, spread it around among two or more institutions, depositing no more than $60,000 in each (allowing for interest). Using more than one branch of the same institution will not increase your coverage. However, there are other ways to increase your coverage: eligible joint deposits and RRSP deposits are insured separately. Each name or group of names is entitled to as much as $60,000 coverage for eligible deposits. Investments not eligible include debentures, foreign currency accounts, stocks, mutual funds, mortgages, treasury bills, and most bonds.

- interest income is fully taxable each year when held outside of an RRSP
- available at most financial institutions
- similar in structure and buying strategies to a term deposit
- cannot be traded; early redemption may be impossible or may involve penalties
- low minimums and limits, which are set by the institutions issuing them
- usual term is one to five years

Government bonds

- these bonds are a way of lending the government money for a fixed interest rate
- interest income is fully taxable each year when held outside of an RRSP
- a safe and easy investment

- available at most financial institutions
- set at a fixed interest rate
- can be traded, resulting in a taxable capital gain or loss

Corporate bonds

- these bonds are issued by a company and are a way of lending that company a fixed sum of money for a fixed amount of time at a fixed interest rate
- interest income is fully taxable each year when held outside of an RRSP
- can be safe or risky, depending on the company issuing the bond
- usually purchased through stock brokers
- usually easy to cash
- can be traded, resulting in a taxable capital gain or loss

Mortgages

- this type of investment lends money to a person or a pool of people to finance their homes, and is secured by the value of the property
- interest income is fully taxable each year when held outside of an RRSP
- safe or risky depending on the borrower
- have fixed or variable interest rates
- can be difficult to sell, however, a sale could trigger a taxable capital gain or loss

Strip bonds

(also called separately traded residual and interest payments, strip coupons, zero coupons, and term investment growth receipts)

- safer if government bonds rather than corporate bonds are involved
- bought at a "discounted" price, it yields the full amount at maturity
- deemed interest income is fully taxable each year when held outside of an RRSP (this is a complex topic — contact a financial advisor for more information)
- redeemable for a set amount at a future date (up to 30 years later)
- can be traded, resulting in a taxable capital gain or loss

Types of Equities

Common and preferred shares

Equity investments are more volatile than fixed income investments because the demand and supply for shares that determines their market value can be influenced by a number of factors. Share prices rise and fall with a company's earnings and prospects and the health of the market in general. Many factors are involved: rumours, government regulations, competition, and other developments that are impossible to predict. You hope to profit by selling the shares for more than you paid for them, creating a capital gain. You may also receive dividends — regular payments in cash or shares that give shareholders a piece of the company's profits. If the company has issued preferred shares, they may carry the bulk of the dividend, leaving little or none for common shareholders. The latter, however, get most of the benefit if the company's value rises.

Shares: (also called **stocks**) A share is a portion of the ownership of a company.

Bonds: A bond is a certificate that proves that you have lent a sum of money to a company or a government for a set amount of time at a fixed interest rate.

Common shares: Owning common shares in a company means that you actually own a part of that company. If the company's value on the stock market increases, you will make a profit; if it decreases, you will experience a loss.

Preferred shares: These shares pay a fixed dividend. If the company that issued the shares does poorly, the preferred shareholders are guaranteed to receive the dividend before common shareholders get anything. (If the company does *really* poorly, no one gets anything!) Conversely, if the company does really well, the preferred shareholder gets only the fixed dividend, and usually doesn't share in any "windfall" dividends.

Mutual funds: A mutual fund pools money from thousands of investors. The portfolio manager purchases a diverse portfolio of securities (stocks, bonds, and money market instruments, etc.) on behalf of the fund investors according to the fund's objectives. Diversification typically makes this kind of investment less risky than buying individual stocks.

Equities range from quite stable to wildly speculative, but even the safest can be more volatile than most fixed-income instruments. They can be very rewarding (in the long term, equities usually bring the greatest returns), but they can also make you nervous. At the nail-biting end are the penny stocks that rise and fall fast enough to take your breath away — and your money, too.

Remember that the more aggressively you play the stock market, the more hazardous it can be to your investments (and your sleep), especially in the short term. You should keep a cash cushion for emergencies. You need to know what you are doing. If you don't have time to manage your investments, find a financial advisor you trust who can help you build the right mix of investments. If you want to start investing but have little saved or don't have the knowledge to keep up to date, you're probably better off starting with a mutual fund.

Mutual Funds

Everyone knows about mutual funds, but not necessarily how they work. A fund pools money from thousands of investors to invest in a portfolio of securities on behalf of the investors, according to the fund's objectives. The securities can include one or more of the usual categories: stocks, bonds, real estate, money market instruments, or other investments.

This has several advantages. Diversification generally lowers your risk, but it's difficult to buy a variety of things if you don't have much money to invest. However, you can buy units in a mutual fund for as little as $500, and presto — it's diversified. The investment choices are made by full-time professional management teams with years of experience and

MUTUAL FUND POPULARITY

Everybody's doing it — your co-workers, your next-door neighbour, and maybe even your grandmother. But are your capital and rate of return guaranteed? No. Mutual funds are not protected by deposit insurance such as CDIC. You are protected if the mutual fund management company goes under since mutual fund assets are held in trust. The fund trustee would hire a new manager to administer the assets. But remember, there are no performance guarantees. If the value of the fund's holdings drops, the value of your investment drops.

SERVICE CHARGES AND FEES

1) Management Fees
- based on the value and growth of the fund
- about 0.5 to 3 percent of the asset value of the fund for the management and administration of the fund

2) No-load Funds
- units sold without any sales charge or commission fee; watch for higher management fees or hidden costs

3) Front-end Load Funds
- charge a percentage of your total investment at the time of investment, meaning that not all of the money you invest goes into the mutual fund. Generally not more than 5 percent

4) Rear/Back-end Load Funds
- commission is deducted when you redeem your investment — the longer you hold a mutual fund, the lower the redemption fee is. After a designated period, the back-end load usually disappears.

expertise who can thoroughly assess each investment in the portfolio. Fund managers often meet with the people who run the companies they invest in — something few individual investors could hope to do. Global markets can be difficult and risky for individuals; share prices of high-quality stocks may put them out of the reach of the small investor. However, mutual funds give you access to both. They're flexible as well: you can choose a variety of funds, as your needs dictate. Finally, mutual fund investments are not locked in, so you can generally redeem them at any time. The fund manager tracks all your transactions and provides regular statements and the information you need to file your annual income taxes. Of course, all those advantages come at a price. Managers charge a management fee to the fund for their services. In addition, you might pay a "load," or sales commission, to get into or out of many funds.

There are all sorts of mutual funds, offering very diverse investments. Here are a few of the common types.

Money market funds

- aim to provide income, liquidity, and safety of capital through investment in short-term money market vehicles (treasury bills, commercial paper of companies and government, etc.)
- return earned from interest paid on the investments
- low risk

Mortgage funds

- invest in residential and commercial mortgages
- achieve most return from income earned on mortgages and potential return from capital gains
- low risk in the case of residential mortgage funds, mortgage-backed securities, and commercial mortgages

Bond or income funds

- invest in the bonds of governments and privately held or publicly traded corporations
- return results from the interest income on bonds held and on potential capital gains
- low to medium risk, depending on type of issuing companies, governments, interest rate, economic environment, etc.

THE IMPORTANCE OF THE PROSPECTUS

A prospectus, in the investment world, is a document required by securities regulators for an offering of stock or other securities to the public. They're not easy reading, but they do contain important information about the issuer of the stock. For new companies you should consult a professional advisor. Mutual fund companies also issue a prospectus that states the fund's investment objectives, among other important details.

Dividend funds

- provide tax-advantaged dividend income with some possibility of capital growth
- invest in preferred and common shares
- medium risk

Balanced funds

- aim for some safety of principal and a balance between income and capital appreciation
- invest in a mix of stocks and bonds
- return realized from income earned from investments, as well as from capital gains
- medium risk

Equity funds

- medium to high risk, depending on type of stock
- aim to provide capital gains or appreciation
- invest in common shares
- prices can fluctuate in value more widely than other mutual funds
- return is the result of capital gains and income from its dividends

International and global funds

- medium to high risk, depending on objectives of the fund, currency fluctuations, geographic area, etc.
- seek opportunities in international markets that offer the best prospects for growth
- invest in one or more of bonds, equities, and money market assets

Sector (industry) funds

- seek capital gains and above-average returns
- invest in a particular sector or industry
- return results from growth in value of investments
- high risk — vulnerable to swings in the particular industry

Real estate funds

- seek long-term growth through capital appreciation and the reinvestment of income

- are less liquid than other types of funds
- may require investors to give advance notice of redemption
- subject to regular valuation, based on professional appraisals of the properties in the portfolio
- high risk in recent years as a result of the real estate market

Ethical funds

- consider the ethical implications of each investment (e.g., might not invest in companies that profit from alcohol, pornography, tobacco, or armaments or in companies not meeting environmental screens)
- medium to high risk

Labour-sponsored funds

- not mutual funds but venture capital funds, which must be invested in small businesses
- offer tax breaks to investors: the amount is different in each province
- may not be redeemable in the first five to seven years, or may face early redemption penalties depending on provincial legislation
- redemption charges usually apply for a certain period
- high risk, liquidity poor
- governed by provincial legislation; the regulations are different in each province

Index funds

- medium to high risk
- aim is to provide capital gains
- invest in the shares of companies that are included in a particular stock market index in the same proportion (i.e., a Canadian index fund would invest in the companies that make up the Toronto Stock Exchange (TSE) 300 Composite Index; an American Index Fund would invest in the stocks that make up the Dow Jones Industrial Average)
- return is the result of capital gains and income from dividends
- managed so that it always mirrors the exchange index

Summary

Investing in a diversified portfolio is a great way to build assets for a comfortable retirement, but don't forget that even the safest investments carry some risk. You should take advantage of more than one of the many investment vehicles available to you. And remember that investing is an active process: you have to play a part in understanding the various types of investments. Find a financial advisor who can help you build and maintain the right mix of investments over the long term.

QUICK RECAP

1. **All investments carry some risk.**
2. **Review what kinds of investments are suitable for you and your situation.**
3. **Monitor your investments.**

CHAPTER 8

Taxes: Not a Penny More, Not a Penny Less

It's Legal!

Now that we've talked a little bit about how to invest your money, let's talk about how to reduce or defer some of the taxes payable on your investments for that long-term plan, so that you can live the good life for another 40 years or so.

Personal Income Tax

Make up for any lost time by checking out the ways you can reduce your income taxes now. This is especially important if you or your spouse has moved into a different tax bracket since the last time you did your taxes. A financial advisor can tell you exactly what you are eligible for. By working together, you can find ways to get the most out of tax deductions and credits. Following are a few benefits you might be interested in:

- **Spousal credit**: Depending on the income of your spouse, you may be eligible for a tax credit.
- **Education and tuition credit**: If your spouse attended school full time in this year and doesn't need to use all of the credit to reduce taxes to zero, you can claim the leftover amount as a credit.
- **Education and tuition credits transferred from a child**: If your child does not require the education and tuition credit to reduce tax to zero, you can claim the unused portion.
- **Disability credit**: You can also receive a disability credit for supporting your spouse if he or she doesn't need to claim it.
- **Medical expense credits**: This credit is based on total expenses exceeding 3 percent of your net income, so it makes sense for the spouse who earns less to claim all of the medical expenses for your family.
- **Infirm dependants over 18**: If you have an infirm child who is over 18 years old, you can receive a credit for the cost of the care of your child.
- **Equivalent-to-spouse exemption**: A single parent can claim the equivalent-to-spouse amount for a dependent child who is under 18. This amount can also be claimed by singles in other situations, so ask a financial advisor if you are single and have any relative living with you who depends on your income.
- **Charitable donations credit**: Now that you have more money than when you were raising a young family and paying off your first assets, you might find yourself contributing to registered charities. Whenever you donate — to your alma mater, international aid organizations, or medical research societies — remember to keep the receipt for your income tax return.
- **Childcare deduction**: If you pay for childcare in your home or your child goes to daycare or even a summer camp, the spouse with the lower income can claim up to $5,000 in tax deductions per child under age 7, and $3,000 for children ages 7 to 16. The caregiver must provide receipts and a social insurance number in order for you to claim the credit — beware of under-the-table operations.
- **Investment counsel or management fees deduction**: The fees that you pay for professional financial counselling services are tax-deductible — yet another reason to use a financial advisor!

Preparing for Tax Time

Nobody likes tax time. It's about as much fun as a trip to the dentist, except that if you skip your dental checkup you're not breaking the law. Given that taxes are inevitable, here are some tips for making tax time almost breezy.

Make sure you've kept all relevant documents throughout the year. These documents include T4s, T5s, charitable tax receipts, T4RSPs, and the notice of assessment the government sends you after you've filed. Your notice of assessment contains useful tidbits, such as your RRSP limit for the current tax year. Keep all documents pertaining to your income tax for six years from the date of filing. Since no accordion folder can stretch that much, put slips, receipts, and other documents into suitably marked envelopes after you've filed your tax return. Put these envelopes in a bigger envelope with the year on it.

If you're self-employed

You also must keep every scrap of paper that has to do with expenses, meaning everything from the bill for your new pickup if you're a house renovator, to receipts for rubber noses if you're a clown. On the income side, no matter how you're paid, you must keep an honest record of these sums.

If you're self-employed, an accountant who is familiar with your industry can save you untold grief, not to mention money. (Ask people in your field to recommend someone.)

Taxing Investments

One of the predictable ironies of investing is that the better you do, the better the government does. Every gain you make through your investment dollar is taxed by the government, but different kinds of investment gains are taxed differently. Here's how it breaks down:

Interest

Interest income — for example, money you earn on debt instruments such as bonds and GICs — is fully taxed. That is, if your marginal tax rate (your "tax bracket") is 50 percent, and you earn $1,000 in interest, then you'll pay the government $500 of that in tax.

Dividends

Dividends from Canadian companies are taxed differently than income from other sources. A dividend is an amount paid by a corporation to shareholders as a form of profit-sharing, and since the corporation has already paid tax on that income, the government has devised a tax credit system to reduce double taxation. The dividend received is increased by 25 percent, but there is a combined federal and provincial tax credit of approximately 20 percent of the grossed-up dividend of a Canadian corporation. For example, consider what happens when someone in the 50 percent tax bracket gets a $1,000 dividend. The dividend is grossed up to $1,250, so the tax is 50 percent of that, or $625. But there is also a tax credit of $250, so the total tax paid is $625 minus $250, or $375.

Capital gains

A capital gain (or loss) is the difference between the buying price and the selling price of an investment. If you make a capital gain on an investment, three quarters (75 percent) of the gain is taxable and it is taxed at your marginal tax rate. A capital loss can offset a capital gain, so get advice on timing if you are selling investments.

Other types of tax shelters

There are other, more exotic types of tax shelters, such as tax credits related to the film industry, that you are bound to hear about. Be cautious with these shelters and don't get involved unless you have received thorough professional advice.

Summary

We all have to pay taxes, but the amount you pay can be drastically reduced with some smart planning, such as using of all your tax credits and investing in an RRSP. These aren't illegal loopholes and you're not cheating the tax system, you're taking advantage of programs that the government set up for you to use. As well, don't forget that you pay tax on your total income, including the income you receive from your investments. Different investments are taxed at different rates, so bear this in mind when doing your tax planning. Be sure to talk to a financial advisor about the tax implication of any major life event (such as a birth, death, marriage, or divorce).

QUICK RECAP

1. **Make sure you and your spouse take advantage of the tax credits for common-law or married couples.**
2. **Your investments are taxable — be sure you know what rate of tax you pay on which investments.**
3. **A financial advisor can guide you to tax breaks you may not find on your own.**

CHAPTER 9

Good Debt, Bad Debt

Managing Your Debt

A common rule followed by personal financial advisors is that your debt-to-income ratio — that is, your monthly debt divided by the amount of your income — should not exceed 35 percent. Count as debt the monthly payments on your rent or mortgage, auto loans, and the minimum monthly balance on your credit cards. Count as income your monthly income before taxes. To calculate the percentage, divide the debt figure by the income figure.

Good debt, bad debt

Good debt is debt that you use to make money — to make an investment, to make an RRSP contribution, to renovate your house to increase its value, to take a training course that will increase your employment income. When you borrow to make an investment, the interest is tax deductible if the loan proceeds are invested in a vehicle that generates income. This does not apply to loans taken out to make an RRSP contribution; the interest on these loans is not tax deductible. Bad debt is the kind that you incur without getting anything valuable in return. High-cost debt is also bad debt. Maxing out your credit cards to eat at expensive restaurants and bars, to buy countless CDs, or to pay your cell phone bill are all forms of bad debt. This kind of bad debt is double trouble because it also means you haven't budgeted properly and are living beyond your

DEBT MANAGEMENT LIMIT	
IF YOUR MONTHLY INCOME IS:	YOUR MONTHLY DEBT PAYMENT SHOULD NOT EXCEED:
$1,000	$350
1,500	525
2,000	700
2,500	875
3,000	1,050
3,500	1,225
4,000	1,400
4,500	1,575
5,000	1,750
5,500	1,925
6,000	2,100
6,500	2,275
7,000	2,450
7,500	2,625
8,000	2,800
8,500	2,975
9,000	3,150
9,500	3,325
10,000	3,500

means. Carrying a lot of long-term debt means paying a lot of interest charges. Sometimes the interest can add up to many times the amount of the original loan. So look into ways to pay down your debt before it becomes a mountain.

Paying off bad debt

Okay, so you're not perfect and you have managed to acquire bad debt. There are sensible ways to manage that undesirable debt.

- ✔ Prioritize your debts by paying off non-deductible high-interest debt, such as credit card balances and auto loans, before low-interest debt, such as bank loans.
- ✔ See if you are eligible for a credit card with a lower rate of interest and transfer your high-interest balance to the new card. This is where your previous good credit rating will come in handy.
- ✔ Get rid of extra credit cards. After all, how many do you really need? Cut them up, then pay off what you owe! Too many cards invite temptation — if you reach your limit on one card, it is too easy to pull out another.

- ✔ Beware of any retailer credit cards. Retailers charge huge amounts of interest, usually about 28 percent, and they accept most major credit cards, anyway.
- ✔ Consolidate your debts by combining lots of smaller loans into one large one at a lower interest rate. However, be aware that though the interest rate may be lower, you could end up paying more unless you make larger monthly payments. If your required monthly payments are lower, it may take you longer to pay back the debt, which could cost you more in interest in the long run.
- ✔ Consider dipping into your savings account or CSBs to pay off high-interest debt. The after-tax interest you lose on the cash or the bonds can be much less than the money you gain by retiring your unpaid credit card balance.
- ✔ Pull out your expense diary and budget again, and see if you can reduce your spending.
- ✔ Start paying with cash or by debit card. This way, you will know exactly how much you can spend and you will get into the habit of living within your means. Think of a debit card as a kind of plastic chequebook, and note all of your debit card purchases as if you were paying by cheque.
- ✔ Pay off your other, higher-interest loans before you pay off your mortgage. Tax-deductible debt should be paid off last.

Making Debt Work for You

It may sound crazy, but debt can work for you. By handling debt responsibly, you will gain a good credit rating, which can help when you need to finance bigger goals, such as buying a house, a vacation property or that Porsche you've always wanted.

To Buy or Not to Buy?

Big-ticket items call for different strategies that are specific to each purchase and are unlike routine expense management. You can buy, rent, or lease. Each choice has its consequences. To buy, you may need to borrow. Things you should consider before you decide to buy:

- depreciation
- rising maintenance costs

- inflation (good for the value of your house, but a problem if you're living on a fixed retirement income)
- cost-benefit (Could you put that money to work in a better investment?)

Leasing versus Buying

Rather than buy, you can lease. Leasing involves a small down payment and a clean break at the end. For a car, that's the way to go, right? Think twice. Leasing used to be sold, possibly oversold, on its tax benefits and its supposed financial superiority. For most people, the income tax break is now small, or nothing at all. Revenue Canada put car leasing on a fairly even basis with conventional financing in 1991, and in 1997 drastically reduced the dollar limit on car leases. Any sales tax advantage disappears if you want to own a vehicle at the end of the lease — and chances are you will. The same applies to the low asset value on which lease financing is based. That only applies if you end up with no asset. Think about what your retirement expenses will be. Do you really want to be spending money on a lease? Or would you be better off buying now, so you don't have to pay for it later? Above all, don't let leasing tempt you to live beyond your means. Other leasing advantages are questionable. The more extravagant claims, the ones that may linger in the back of your mind, were made when leasing companies kept their information close to the vest. Faced with disclosure legislation in British Columbia and other provinces, they became more open, and less aggressive in their claims. Interest rates may be lower than elsewhere, but don't count on it. Leasing software is now available to let you perform the same calculations the companies make and compare a prospective lease with other means of financing.

Look before you lease

Leasing leaves you with nothing at the end except an option to buy. If you walk away, you've done yourself out of an asset. On top of that, there may be repair costs to bring a vehicle up to the leasing company's projected end-of-lease value, and/or a distance charge for too many kilometres driven. Coming up to retirement, you probably want your wheels to be your own, debt-free and with plenty of distance left in them. If you lease, your monthly payment is based on:

- the price of the item;
- the interest rate charged by the leasing company;

- the anticipated resale (residual) value of the item at the end of the lease;
- the length of the lease (usually two to four years); and
- the down payment you make (if any).

Here are some benefits to leasing:

- There is a minimal down payment, if any.
- Monthly payments are usually lower than if you purchased the item using a bank loan.
- It is easier to be approved for a lease than for a bank loan.
- There are cash flow advantages to leasing.

Leasing has its disadvantages, as well:

- At the end of the lease you have nothing to show for it — you haven't added to your assets.
- If you want low monthly payments you may have to make a down payment.
- To lower those payments you may have to accept a higher residual value at the end of the lease. You have to pay that amount if you want to buy the item. If you don't, you must hope that someone else will pay it. If not, you may be responsible for the shortfall.
- If the leasing company gets more than the residual value when it sells the returned asset, you will not benefit.

As you get closer to retiring, leasing's disadvantages increasingly outweigh its benefits.

Finding the Money

Remember Beth and John from Chapter 2? Well, they'd like to upgrade their kitchen. The renovation will cost about $50,000. They'd prefer to wait on getting started, since they haven't had any time to save up for it. Between the two of them, they have only $4,000 saved that isn't earmarked for either their emergency fund or their RRSP contributions. With their retirement years right around the corner, it might not be a great idea to put out such a large chunk of money, but their heart is set on it. What should they do?

Be Your Own Guarantor

Rather than go into debt on retirement's doorstep, you may be tempted to cash in some of your savings, such as Canada Savings Bonds, for a major purchase. It's not a good idea, since you won't be able to live off the kitchen renovation the way you would off the savings bonds. However, you can use your assets as collateral for a loan. You'll get the best possible rate because the collateral is risk-free. When the loan is repaid, your savings will still be intact. It's important to protect your nest egg at this stage of your life, so don't succumb to trading security for luxuries.

Financing Your Purchases by Borrowing

Alright: so you've taken your retirement needs into consideration, but you still can't pass up that all-terrain vehicle, or that complete kitchen renovation. You've decided to buy right away. After going through your budget you may have decided that part of your earnings can go toward the purchase without harming your RRSP. The rest you'll have to borrow.

Credit Cards

Chances are, you've had credits cards for a long time. If you've avoided them to now, you're a rare creature. There are different types, and by now you've probably settled on what kind of card you like to carry, but if you're thinking of upgrading to a gold or platinum card, decide what extras suit your needs. Features you may consider valuable include

- prepaid insurance on rental cars;
- extended warranties on purchases;
- protection in case of unauthorized use of your card; and
- bonus points that can be redeemed for merchandise.

THE IMPORTANCE OF HAVING GOOD CREDIT

Your credit rating sums up your reputation as a borrower. It evaluates your debt in the past six years and in the present. Banks, mortgage lenders, credit card companies, potential employers, landlords, and anyone else with a legitimate interest in your financial reliability can look up your rating to decide whether you are a good risk. That's why it's so important to look after it. At this stage in your life, if you have a bad credit rating, it probably reflects poor money management habits. Good thing you're reading this book!

Are you a responsible user?

Making purchases on a credit card is the simplest way of borrowing money. The minimum monthly payment you're required to make on your balance looks so forgiving — only 5 percent or so. It hardly feels like borrowing — but there's almost nowhere you can borrow money at a more expensive rate. Check these guidelines. If you're already following them, you can rest easy:

- When you receive your bill, pay the full amount each month on time.
- Avoid cash advances. Interest on a cash advance is calculated from the very first day you borrow the cash.
- Save your receipts and keep track of your spending — even credit card companies make mistakes.
- Call your credit card company immediately if your card is stolen.

What Kind of Loan Do You Need? ?

Before you go out to get a loan for a major purchase, you should consider the alternatives.

Fixed-rate versus variable-rate instalment loans

Two of the most common types of loans are fixed-rate instalment loans and variable-rate instalment loans. With a fixed-rate instalment loan the term and the interest rate are set when you get the loan and they do not change. The monthly payments are a combination of the principal repayment and the interest, and because they never change, you always know how much to budget for. A variable-rate instalment loan differs from a fixed-rate instalment loan because it reflects fluctuating interest rates. A variable-rate loan is pegged at a specified percentage

CREDIT CARD FEES AND INTEREST

Shop around for a credit card. They vary widely in terms of the annual fees and interest rates they charge, and the frills they offer. For example, interest rates for different types of cards from one leading international card company range from 8.4 to 18.5 percent, annual fees range from zero to $100, and available features include free rental car insurance and a 1 percent rebate on all of your purchases. A card that covers your travel health insurance costs can easily pay for itself if you travel to the United States frequently, even if the annual fee is quite steep.

above the prime lending rate, and the interest that you pay will fluctuate with changes in the prime rate. You repay the same principal amount from month to month, but your interest will vary. With a variable-rate loan you will save money if interest rates decline, but it will take longer to pay back your loan if interest rates rise.

Demand loans

Demand loans are quite risky. With a demand loan, the lender usually sets a repayment schedule covering the term of the loan before lending the money, but the lender can also demand that the money be paid back in full at any time. This is known as "calling" a loan, and can have very serious consequences for your finances if your loan is called without advance warning.

Lines of credit

A personal line of credit is the most common and convenient type of variable-rate loan. Once you are approved for a line of credit, you can access it at any time, up to the pre-determined limit, with special cheques or a credit card. A normal line of credit starts at about $5,000. Many people find it convenient to pay for high-ticket items, such as home improvements, vacations, computer equipment, or investments, with a line of credit. The terms of repayment are set in advance and the interest rates can be better than those on an unpaid credit card balance.

There are two different types of lines of credit: secured and unsecured. A secured line of credit, such as a second mortgage, offers collateral for the loan and usually has a lower interest rate. An unsecured line of credit is not backed by collateral and usually carries a higher interest rate.

Summary

Although the word *debt* has a negative sound to it, debts are not always bad. It's virtually impossible to live in our society without incurring debts — such as a mortgage or car payments — and debt can actually be a good thing if it improves your net worth. If you are financially responsible, there is no need to shy away from debt, but remember that your creditors are running a business, and aren't lending you money out of the goodness of their hearts. Be aware of how much interest your various creditors are charging you, and always opt for loans with the lowest interest rates possible.

QUICK RECAP

1. **There is good debt and bad debt — use good debt to acquire assets that increase your net worth.**
2. **Leasing has some advantages over buying, but those decrease as you approach retirement.**
3. **Take care of your credit rating. It stays with you for seven years.**
4. **For most people, a secured line of credit is the lowest-interest-rate type of loan available.**

CHAPTER 10

On Golden Pond?

Renting versus Buying a Home

As you approach retirement, you might want to get rid of the family home and find cozier digs more befitting your impending years of relaxation. Deciding whether to rent or buy is something you'll be considering (and you thought you were done with all that). Ownership is appealing. You'll have the cash if you sell the old place, and why pay rent when you could trade one equity for another? But mortgage interest does nothing for equity. Add up the annual costs of ownership, including interest, taxes, maintenance, insurance, heat, and utilities, and subtract the amount your mortgage is reduced over a year. The result is the non-recoverable cost of owning your own home. If you can rent comparable accommodation for less, you may be better off to invest the difference in your RRSP. One thing to remember, though, is that most investment profits are taxed. Capital gains on the value of your principal residence are not. If you are confident that your new residence will appreciate in value, that gain —

if there is one — will be tax-free. However, in some areas of the country in today's marketplace, real estate is not a sound investment if all you're trying to do is increase your worth. Consider renting if any of the following applies to you:

- You can't afford the large down payment along with all the other up-front costs of buying property.
- You can't afford the additional costs (including CMHC insurance) that a small down payment would require.
- Housing prices are peaking — it's a sellers' market — and renting is a short-term solution.

Maggie's dilemma

Maggie, whom we met earlier, is renting a condo for $1,250 a month, but the owner is putting pressure on her to buy it. The condominium fee is $250 a month, and the taxes are $1,500 a year. She has $20,000 she can use as a down payment. Is it worth it for her to buy? Can she invest her money at a higher rate of return than the cost of her rent? It depends on the purchase price and on investment rates of return. She should look at the monthly cost of buying the condo, and compare it to the cost of renting. In scenario 1, the purchase price is $150,000 and interest rates are 5.75 percent. If she takes out a 15-year mortgage, her monthly payment will be $1,080. Add to that the condo fee of $250 a month and taxes of $125 a month, and her monthly costs will be $1,455, or $205 a month more than the rent she had been paying. As well, she will be losing the 4.4 percent interest (after tax) she currently gets on the $20,000 she would use as down payment, which is $73 a month in income she will lose, so the increased cost is $278 a month. But from the very first month of her mortgage, she would be paying the principal of the mortgage down by $457, so she would be increasing her net worth by over $450 a month, at an increased cost of $278 a month. If she can afford the increased monthly cost, buying the condo is a good investment for her. Scenario 2 in the table shows the opposite case, where an increased purchase price and higher interest rate make it advantageous to rent.

COST-BENEFIT ANALYSIS CALCULATOR

	FACTOR	SCENARIO 1	SCENARIO 2
Start with the:	Purchase price	$150,000	$200,000
And the:	Interest rate	5.75%	7.50%
And use a spreadsheet or mortgage calculator to calculate your:	Monthly mortgage payment	$1,080	$1,669
Add in the:	Condo fee	$250	$250
And the:	Taxes/month	$125	$125
And you have your:	Total monthly cost of buying	$1,455	$2,044
Compare this to the:	Rent	$1,250	$1,250
And calculate the:	Cost of buying minus cost of renting	$205	$794
Add the:	After-tax monthly income not received on the money used for down payment	$73	$73
To get:	Net effect on personal cash flow	$278	$867
Go back to the spreadsheet or mortgage calculator and look up the:	Principal paid off per month	$457	$544
Compare these last two numbers to get the number you are interested in:	Monthly cost advantage of buying	$179	
	Monthly cost advantage of renting		$323

Assumes investments at 8% compounded monthly; 45% tax bracket.

When You Buy a House or Vacation Property

As we said above, when you decide to buy another home or a vacation property, don't invest with profit in mind. That's nice if you get it, but far from predictable. If it doesn't happen, you could spend a long time in the wrong dwelling, waiting for the market to change. Assuming your choice is financially prudent, you should decide on a place because that's where you want to live, and because its features will serve you well for the foreseeable future. Those criteria should guide you at any age, but the older you are, the less time you may want to spend waiting for a poor choice to turn into a better one. Also, think about whether this is the right time to do it. Do you have the finances to buy what you want, or will you have to settle for a "fixer-upper" that you can't afford to fix? You may own the place, but it also owns a piece of you. Freehold property requires your regular — even constant — attention. Condominium and other property with shared elements require maintenance fees that are out of your direct control. The costs of buying and selling property can be significant. Consider real estate commissions, legal fees, GST, land transfer tax, and moving costs.

Capitalizing on Your Mortgage

You probably thought you'd never deal with a mortgage again. And if you're "downsizing" from a family home to a smaller residence, you might not have to get another mortgage (you might even be enjoying a tax-free profit), but, then again, maybe you'll have to. Remember that a mortgage can do more for you than simply finance your home. Mortgages can be used to:

- purchase or build a second home
- finance renovations
- consolidate your debts
- start a business
- finance other purchases, such as a new car, or a vacation property

Because they are well-secured, real estate mortgages carry lower interest rates than any other type of loan available to you but may incur more substantial fees. This advantage makes them particularly attractive as financing for something other than a home, since low rates are harder to find for cars and furniture, unless you lock yourself into an expensive lease. At the same time, mortgages at favourable rates are not usually available for smaller amounts. A mortgage typically involves a large principal to be repaid over many years. This is a major financial commitment, and not one to be entered into lightly.

There are costs to setting up and registering a mortgage — part of the extra chunk of money you must be prepared to come up with on closing the real estate deal. However, second mortgages are often in the form of a secured line of credit — so you get a cheque book (see Chapter 9 for more details on lines of credit).

Getting approved

Lenders will want to look at your finances first. Besides your credit rating, they will consider whether you can afford the monthly mortgage payments along with household costs and your other obligations. They consider your debt-to-income ratio, which is the percentage that mortgage payments, property taxes, and heating take out of your income.

Insurance for your mortgage

Your home is one of your most valuable assets, but if you or your spouse were to die, would your family be able to keep up the mortgage payments? If not, they would be in danger of losing their home. You can avoid that risk by choosing one of these options:

- **Buy personal life insurance.** The policy proceeds are paid directly to the beneficiary, who can use them for any purpose. Your family can pay off the mortgage or continue the periodic mortgage payments while deciding what to do over the long term.
- **Buy mortgage life insurance.** Available through most mortgage lenders, it's a specially designed term policy that pays off the balance of your mortgage to the lending institution if you die. The premiums are tacked on to your regular mortgage payments.

Before you arrange your mortgage, ask yourself whether you will be able to carry it for the full term. You may be in your prime earning years now, but will the mortgage be paid off before you retire? Remember, you want to have as few financial responsibilities as possible once you reach retirement. Tailor the term, and therefore the size of the mortgage, accordingly.

Borrowing Mortgage Money from Your RRSP

Who better to borrow from than yourself? If you have money locked away in a self-directed RRSP, you can finance your own mortgage. This means that the payments you make will be to your own benefit, and you can set the rate (within limits) to favour your own goals — to increase your tax-sheltered savings, or to get your mortgage paid down as quickly as possible. The limits, however, are fairly tight — no sweet deals are permitted; the rate and other terms must be within the current market. There are other restrictions that create extra costs: you will have to pay for special mortgage insurance and added RRSP administration charges, both initial and annual. If your spouse's RRSP is also used, some or all of those costs could be doubled. For that and other reasons, it pays to make a cost comparison with conventional borrowing. Often the costs associated with this process exceed the benefit.

Summary

Retirement is often a time when people move — from a large family home to a condo, or to a quiet country home. Keep that in mind as you plan for your retirement. No matter where you might move to, remember that owning and renting both have their benefits. If you already own a home and are thinking of fulfilling your dream of buying a vacation property, you may be closer to that goal than you think: you can use your mortgage on your first home to help finance your second, or you can lend yourself mortgage money from your RRSP.

QUICK RECAP

1. Use the cost-benefit analysis calculator to determine which is better for you: renting or buying.
2. Buying a vacation home can be a great reward, but think of the responsibilities, too.
3. You can use the mortgage on a house you already own to finance your vacation home.

CHAPTER 11

Family Financial Planning

Have Your Circumstances Changed? ?

The last time you sat down and really thought about your circumstances and how they may have changed was probably when you tied the knot. Or when you pinned your first diaper. But a lot may have changed since then. You may have had more kids, or you may now be single or remarried. You are probably facing caring for your aging parents, and are starting to worry about whether your kids will do the same for you. And you're occupied with the thought of retiring, either on your own, or together with your spouse. No matter how your family situation has changed since you brought home your first paycheque, your finances have probably changed with it. Whether you have moved, inherited another property, lost that property to a divorce, or merged properties through a remarriage, your changes in assets and family responsibilities (read expenses) will have a dramatic effect on how you manage your finances. Although everyone's family situation is unique, this chapter will cover some of the more common changes people in their forties, fifties, and sixties encounter, and will show you some ways of dealing with those changes.

Yours or Ours?

Whether you have stayed married or you've remarried, consider the financial implications of your life as a couple. Are you both happy with the way you divide up expenses and assets, or is one of you shouldering too much of the burden? If you are paying alimony to a former spouse, you may not be able to afford half the expenses. If you have just had a promotion and a raise, it may be time for you to offer to pay more than half the expenses. Or if you've been downsized, you may want your partner to cover your half for a while.

MARRIAGE MEANS REASSESSMENT

If you're getting married, remarried, or starting to live together, you probably want to get things right.

It is important to identify what you and your partner own, both jointly and separately. Here are some suggestions to make your joint financial life a success.

- Draft an upfront agreement (consult a lawyer if you feel you need to).
- Redraft your will and check your beneficiary designations on RRSPs and life insurance.
- Be honest about any debts or financial responsibilities that you have, including alimony and child support from previous relationships.
- Talk about what kind of lifestyle you both want. (What's your definition of a luxury?)

The Financial Aftermath of Divorce

Divorce is stressful both emotionally and financially, so this is a good time to let a professional take some of the burden from you. Call a family lawyer, your financial advisor, and perhaps a tax advisor in addition to your friends and family. With proper support, you can make the process less painful. When dividing your assets from the marriage, get independent legal advice — don't rely on your ex-spouse's financial advisors to counsel you on what is your due. Assets could come to you in various forms:

- You may receive the family home.
- You may receive a lump-sum payment or other assets toward your settlement.

CERTAINTIES OF LIFE

There are good reasons to name your spouse as your beneficiary when you contribute to an RRSP account. However, there could be other costs, so consult your advisor. When you die, your spouse can transfer the funds into his or her RRSP account on a tax-deferred basis. If you leave your RRSPs to your children, parents, or anyone else, the value of the RRSPs will likely be taxed in your name in the year that you die. This is not the case if you have no spouse and the money goes to a financially dependent child or grandchild. You should consult your lawyer about the implications to your estate plan of not naming a spouse as a beneficiary of an RRSP, RRIF, or life insurance policy.

- You may be entitled to a share of the CPP/QPP or workplace pension that your spouse contributed to during the marriage.
- You might be able to share funds accumulated in your spouse's RRSP. The amount you are entitled to will depend on the family property laws of the province where you live. But you should be able to equalize your assets through a transfer: divorce is one of the few instances in which a transfer from one RRSP to another, owned by your spouse or ex-spouse, is allowed. Keep in mind that an RRSP carries a future tax liability (i.e., one dollar in an RRSP is worth somewhat less than one dollar in after-tax assets).

Spousal Support

Both men and women can apply for spousal support. Canada's Divorce Act sets out four objectives for spousal support:

- recognition of the economic advantages and disadvantages to spouses arising from the marriage breakdown;
- apportionment between the spouses of the financial costs of raising children;
- relief of financial hardship; and
- promotion of self-sufficiency.

Courts are now likely to order permanent support for spouses who had been homemakers during the marriage, but the level of support is usually quite low. Some courts do recognize that a homemaker's contributions (not necessarily financial) to a marriage can have lifelong effects on that spouse's earning potential.

Child Support

Federal and provincial governments have recently introduced measures to improve the level of child support and to make sure it is paid. The new regulations state that parents who fall too far behind in their payments could lose their passports. If evaders can't be found, Revenue Canada will open its data banks to help provincial enforcement agencies identify their employers and garnish their wages. Some provinces have more regulations than others, so find out your rights if you've got a deadbeat ex. For agreements signed or varied May 1, 1997, or later, child support is not taxable to the parent who receives it, and it's not deductible for the person who pays it.

Looking Ahead at Education

If you started a family late, you may be considering how to save for your child's education even as you're preparing to retire. You probably know people whose dreams of a university or college education were dashed because they didn't have the money to see it through. That's the kind of disappointment you don't want your children to face. Just as with your own retirement savings, you can take advantage of the power of compound returns. The money you put away every month will eventually grow enough to finance the high cost of education. A mere $100 invested monthly at 8 percent (compounded monthly) can grow to over $40,000 (before taxes) in 15 years. That may still be enough to pay the tuition fees for a typical undergraduate degree at a Canadian university, even if you allow for inflation and taxes.

Child tax benefits

If you receive a monthly child tax benefit, you could put it toward your child's education. Revenue Canada determines the amount and eligibility based on your income, your child's age, and the number of children you have. If you deposit this payment into an account that is in your child's name, the income it earns will be taxed in the child's hands.

Registered education savings plans (RESPs)

RESPs are a popular way to save for higher education. You have several types of plans to choose from, which will invest your money in numerous ways including insured mortgages and deposits, depending on the terms of the plan. To set up an RESP, you make a contribution and name a beneficiary. Although your contributions are not tax deductible, the earnings accumulate tax free until they are withdrawn. When your child attends university, he or she becomes eligible to receive payments from the plan. Income from the plan is taxed in the child's hands. Capital can be returned to the contributor or paid to the beneficiary. In either case, a return of capital is tax-free.

In 1997, the federal government changed the legislation so that if the designated beneficiary does not pursue post-secondary education by the age of 25, the earnings from a plan that you have had for 10 years can be moved into the contributor's RRSP, as long as the amount is not over the contributor's RRSP contribution limit. You also could take the earnings as income, but you will be taxed on them and will have to pay a 20 percent penalty.

Formal trusts for your children's education

As an alternative to an RESP, you might consider establishing trusts with formal written trust agreements to fund your children's education. This can have advantages for income splitting purposes but requires detailed tax planning and advice.

Caring for Aging Parents

Taking responsibility for your aging parents can be emotionally and financially draining, especially if you're still looking after your children's upbringing. Before it's too late, sit down with your siblings, your spouse, and your parents to talk about what kind of financial assistance or care they may need. Will they be able to afford it, or will they expect you to help out? Is that expense built into your savings, or will you have to mortgage your retirement to pay for theirs? Here are some suggested conversation starters:

- Who has power of attorney? (See the next chapter for more on the legal implications of a power of attorney.)
- In case of illness, who is the primary caregiver?
- Whose insurance will cover medical treatment?
- How much money do they need to save to pay for the kind of care they may need? Will the kids be expected to chip in? Too many children don't know enough about their parents' finances when they start caring for them.
- Can they afford the kind of help they may need?

It's a delicate subject, and can raise a lot of sensitive issues. But not talking about it is bound to raise more problems, and it's just avoiding the inevitable. Knowing what your parents want before they need it will make decisions much easier for everyone in the family. We'll continue this discussion in a legal context in the next chapter.

Summary

A family is a micro-economy that needs to be managed well and wisely. If you started a business, you would have a business plan. When planning your future, remember to take into consideration the different stages your family goes through as a whole.

QUICK RECAP

1. Marriage (or divorce) means re-assessment: work out a financial plan that makes both partners happy.
2. Setting up ways to pay for your children's education will give them a head start on their own finances.
3. Be financially prepared for taking care of your aging parents or in-laws.

CHAPTER 12

You Can't Take It with You

Gord and Shelly are in great shape: they reassessed and reorganized their investments, Gord quit smoking, and their daughter moved into an apartment of her own (they miss her company, but they've also noticed a decrease in their monthly expenses — especially the phone bill!). But the one thing they haven't been very diligent about is their estate planning. Like most people, Gord and Shelly don't like talking about death. Even less do they like the idea of broaching the topic of their own deaths with their children. But their recent lessons in financial planning have made Gord and Shelly realize that in order to lessen the financial burden on each other and their family, and to have a healthy inheritance left for their kids, they had better take this crucial step toward security. Gord and Shelly have also agreed to share all of their estate plans with their family so that there will be no stressful surprises to worry about in the event of a death.

Estate Planning – Death and Taxes

Why do we spend so little time planning for the certainties in life? Unless you want to be in trouble with the government, you have to keep your taxes in order. But preparing for the big event — death — is left entirely up to you. Maybe you think that death is the last thing you need to worry about, since once you're gone, it's not your problem, is it? But it will be your family's problem. By creating a solid estate plan, you will ensure that the people you care about are provided for when you're gone. You'll also have peace of mind in knowing that your affairs will be looked after in accordance with your wishes. Estate planning ensures that what you leave behind goes where you want it. If it's done right, you'll be able to transfer and preserve your wealth in an effective and orderly manner. It also avoids needless taxation, delay, probate expenses, and family conflict.

Minimize, Minimize

To maximize the size of your estate for your heirs and to ensure your survivors are properly provided for, your goals are to

- minimize the amount of taxes your heirs must pay on estate assets, and
- minimize the trauma and hassle for your heirs, who need to organize your affairs when grief-stricken about their loss.

Your game plan

- Determine how you want your estate to be distributed upon your death.
- Determine the amount of money required to provide for survivors and dependants, as well as funeral costs and probate fees.
- Consult with your financial advisor to determine if you need insurance.
- Have your lawyer prepare a will to distribute your estate assets.

What you need to plan your estate

- financial plan
- will
- executor
- power of attorney
- guardian (if you still have minor children)

Drafting a Will

A will is a legal document that sets out how you want your assets to be distributed and disposed of (and this spring cleaning gives you the chance to actually see what you own). It also names an executor — the person or corporation (in cases where a trust company acts as the executor) who will administer your estate and distribute your property.

If you don't have a will, provincial law, rather than your wishes, will determine the distribution of your estate. And if you have no relatives at all, the government will get everything you worked so hard for. It's a good idea to hire a lawyer to draw up your will. You can do it yourself, but unless you comply with all the formalities, your will could end up being invalid or not properly specifying what you want to happen to your estate. It could also be subject to misinterpretation, fail to deal with all your property, neglect to take advantage of tax elections, and have other flaws that turn out to be very expensive. Your will should include

- the name of your executor and a description of his or her powers,
- a list of beneficiaries and specific bequests and legacies, and
- terms of any trusts to be established.

Review your will at least every three to five years and at key life events to keep it up to date. Nearly every big change, financial or personal, can change your will. For example, if you are divorced, do you really want your possessions to end up in your ex-spouse's hands? And if you are remarried, your new marriage will void any previous wills you might have. That means your new spouse could end up with the family summer home.

WHO CAN HELP

Here are a few professionals you may want to involve in drafting your will.

- lawyer
- accountant
- financial advisor
- trust company (can work with your lawyer or recommend one)

Granting power of attorney

In case you ever become incapable of managing your own affairs, you will need to ensure someone is in a position to look after your best interests. This is the person to whom you grant power of attorney. If you don't appoint someone before you become incapable of managing your affairs, application will have to be made to a court to grant someone this power. The person you appoint has the power to act on your behalf in all financial affairs, potentially to make health care decisions for you and to sign your legal documents. The person you appoint should be trustworthy, competent, objective, and familiar with your financial affairs, so for most people, a spouse is the ideal candidate. You can change or terminate the power of attorney at any time.

It's a good idea to specify an enduring power of attorney. This will allow the person you appoint to act on your behalf if you become mentally incompetent. An enduring power of attorney remains in effect until you die. At that time, control of your estate passes to the executor named in your will.

What happens if you don't have a will?

If you die without making a will, provincial law dictates how your assets will be distributed. In most provinces the majority of your assets go to your spouse, with your child or children receiving a percentage of your estate. However, in some provinces the deceased's assets are divided equally between the spouse and children.

Naming a guardian for minor children

Choosing a guardian to raise your children if you and your spouse die is a practical but difficult decision. When trying to decide who might be a good guardian, think over these questions:

- Will this person be able to care for the children until they reach the age of 18 (at the very least)?
- Does this person share your values and goals for your children?
- Is this person willing to shoulder the responsibility?
- Does this person have a good relationship with your children?

Although you may have stated your preference for a guardian in your will, the court has the power to make the final decision if there are reasons to believe the person you have chosen will not act in the best interests of the children. But in most cases the court will respect your choice.

What if you haven't appointed a guardian for your children? The surviving spouse gets the children. If both parents die, someone has to apply to the courts to be appointed the children's guardian, which takes time and money. You don't want to put people through that — so you should appoint a guardian, just in case.

Setting Up a Testamentary Trust

Trusts are one way of dealing with your assets after you die. They come with income-tax opportunities and burdens, depending on your circumstances. You need a lawyer to help you with this. Your property is transferred into the testamentary trust on your death. It is managed by a "trustee," who is responsible for carrying out the terms of the trust. There are many ways to use trusts, to provide for both minor and adult heirs.

Select a trustee

To create a trust to take effect upon your death, the trust is included as a provision of your will. There are two kinds of trustees: corporate trustees, such as a trust company; or individual trustees, such as a family member, lawyer, or friend. The position of trustee comes with a lot of responsibility. Appointing a family member is one possibility. A corporate trustee is also an option.

HELPFUL HINT

To protect minors, your will can establish a trust for their legacies. If you're concerned about the free-spending habits of your heirs, you can set out a plan for paying their inheritance in instalments.

Make an Estate Plan

Without an estate plan, you won't even know what will be left over for your beneficiaries. Here are the basic elements that your plan should have:

1. Determine the value of your estate. Look at the net worth statement you prepared in Chapter 2. Your assets should include any lump-sum benefits from your company pension plan, CPP/QPP, and life insurance.

2. Anticipate your estate's liabilities:
   - **Funeral costs** (you can prepay them by putting the money in a trust where it can earn some interest)
   - **Executor or administrator fee** (3 to 5 percent of the estate value)
   - **Legal fees** (should be less than 2 percent of the estate value)
   - **Probate fees** (court fees vary from province to province, but are based on the value of the estate)
   - **Trustee fees**
   - **Taxes** (capital gains taxes don't apply to assets that are transferred to your surviving spouse, but everything else is deemed to be sold at the date of death; three quarters of the capital gain is taxable on your final tax return; the principal-residence exemption still applies and special provisions are available for certain farm property and some shares of Canadian-controlled private corporations)
3. Subtract your costs from the value of your estate to determine what you will be leaving to your beneficiaries.

HELPFUL HINT

You can minimize your probate fees by removing assets from your estate, but there are certain risks to doing so. **Be sure to consult a professional advisor first!** There are two ways to do this: Register property or bank accounts jointly so that they automatically pass through to the survivor, although this means sharing ownership and control of the asset during your lifetime. Designate beneficiaries to your insurance, RRSPs, and RRIFs. Caution: there can be tax and other consequences associated with adding an individual as a joint owner of capital property, as well as designating that individual as beneficiary.

Life Insurance

You may not be able to outsmart death, but there are ways to lessen the blow to the family you have left behind. If you have dependants, try to imagine what would happen to them if you were to die. Your family could be in dire financial straits within months or even weeks if you haven't foreseen how they'll replace the lost income. And what about ongoing payments? The mortgage on the house? Daycare costs while your spouse works? Plans for your children's education? All these are at risk if you don't have enough life insurance. What is life insurance intended to do?

- It provides your beneficiaries with replacement income (some expenses, such as daycare, housekeeper, and home repairs may increase).
- It creates an estate to carry through your goals for the future (support and education of children, future allocations for spouse, charitable causes, etc.).
- It protects the assets you've acquired so that they won't have to be sold to pay outstanding debts, such as a mortgage or the capital gains taxes accrued on your investments.
- It covers death expenses and debts.

What do you need?

Singles

If you are single and without dependants or significant debt, you probably don't need life insurance. Your money may be better invested in a regular savings program. You probably want to ensure that you have enough money to cover such depressing expenses as a funeral and burial plot should you die. If you have sizable debts, you might consider buying term insurance (see below).

Families

If you still have a young family, you are in the greatest need of protection. If you are a wage earner, life insurance equal to at least 10 times your income is a good starting point. A $300,000 life insurance policy would provide an income of about $32,500 a year for 15 years (assuming an annual interest rate of 8 percent).

Don't overlook the need for life insurance for a stay-at-home parent. High-quality childcare and domestic help can be very expensive.

What's your type?

No matter what kind of insurance you buy, the premiums will be based on four factors:

- age
- health
- coverage amount
- length of coverage

Ask your financial advisor to help you do a proper needs analysis. Factor in all of your current expenses, plus the replacement of the lost income and saving for retirement. Remember to allow for inflation.

Term Insurance

A term plan provides protection for a set length of time — usually one, five, ten, or twenty years. Should you die during that period, your term policy will pay a specified amount to the beneficiaries you name.

Term insurance is the most affordable kind of life insurance, so it's a good buy for young families. You can usually renew your term when it's up. But though the premiums may seem pretty affordable in the beginning, they will increase with each policy renewal. As long as you pay the premiums, your insurance company can't deny you renewal because you've developed health problems. But most term policies do not allow you to renew after age 75 or 80, by which time the premiums would be very expensive. You usually have the option of converting the policy to one of the company's permanent insurance products, without having to prove that you are in good health. But sometimes the costs of converting can be high, so you may wish to investigate the cost of switching to a different policy.

Permanent Insurance

This insurance covers you for as long as you live. It renews automatically for your entire lifetime, provided you continue to pay the premiums. The most common types of permanent insurance are whole life and universal life.

Whole life

Whole life insurance offers a guaranteed amount of insurance coverage for life, as well as a cash value fund that keeps the premium costs level. Premiums are fixed and guaranteed for a set number of years or for life. However, whole life policies are more expensive than term policies.

The cash value is a tax-sheltered savings fund. If you want to borrow the cash value, you have to pay interest, and the death benefits will be reduced unless the loan is paid back. The growth in the cash value can give you additional options, such as extended coverage or lower premium payments.

Universal life

Universal life also provides insurance coverage for life, combining a self-directed savings portfolio with insurance. The difference is that in whole life the cash value fund is invested as the insurance company sees fit, whereas in universal life you get a say in how it is invested. Any gain on the withdrawals you make from the savings portion are taxed and the plan could be subject to surrender charges if you cash it in. If you borrow against the policy, that amount may be charged interest and the proceeds will be reduced unless the loan is paid back.

Disability Insurance

It's easy to feel invincible when you are young and healthy. But, chances are, you or someone close to you may become disabled at some point. If you are ill, injured, or permanently disabled, where will your income come from?

Your employer

The benefits from an employer-sponsored plan are taxable if the employer paid the premiums, which is why even a generous amount of income replacement could dwindle after taxes. If your employer contributes to the worker's compensation plan, you could receive coverage if you are injured on the job. This compensation is not taxable, but you'll still need additional coverage in case you are injured off the work site or become ill.

The government

You're probably well aware that government insurance isn't exactly generous. So it's never wise to rely solely on government insurance. The Canada/Quebec Pension Plan pays a small monthly pension. It applies to those who have contributed to the plan for a minimum of two to five years if the disability is "severe and prolonged." The pension is made up of two parts: a flat-rate amount and an amount based on how much and for how long you paid into the CPP/QPP. But the total is minimal — the most you can expect is about $850 a month. As well, you'll have to wait between 12 and 24 months to receive your benefits.

Employment Insurance (EI) also pays disability benefits, but the amount is limited, you must qualify, and your benefits are taxable.

Private disability insurance

You can buy as much private insurance as you think you'll need, and the benefits can be tax-free. Group plans are less expensive than individual plans, but they will pay only up to 65 percent of your income, which also includes any government or employer benefits you receive. Keep a lookout for plans that pay back some of your money if you don't make a claim. The premiums are more expensive, but if you are in good health, they may be worth your while. Individual plans can be customized to suit your needs and can be designed to supplement any EI or group coverage you already have. When shopping for a private disability plan, ask these questions:

- Is this a group or individual plan?
- Can I afford the premiums? If not, what alternatives do I have?
- What is the definition of "disabled"?
- What circumstances are excluded from the plan?
- How long is the waiting period before benefits are paid out?
- How long will the benefits be paid?
- What happens to premium payments while I'm disabled?
- Is there inflation protection?
- If I don't claim insurance, will I get any money back?

Critical Illness Insurance

This type of policy pays out a sum of money if you contract a specified illness, such as cancer or Multiple Sclerosis. You can use the proceeds to pay for treatment, subsidize your income, take a vacation, or for whatever purpose you want.

Summary

To ensure that your estate is distributed smoothly, you need to start preparing for the inevitable now. Once you've set up your plan, review it annually. Seek professional advice to ensure you're doing things right the first time. A poorly designed will can only add to a family's grief.

If you lose your spouse, you'll be grateful for estate planning because you won't have to spend time unravelling a financial nightmare. You'll be able to focus on the emotional needs of your family, and you can start thinking about rebuilding your life from the bedrock of sound finances. There is nothing worse than another surprise after a death in the family. Make a will.

QUICK RECAP

1. **Make a will.**
2. **Review your estate plan regularly.**
3. **Re-evaluate your will every three to five years to keep it up to date with changes in your life.**
4. **Ensure that you're adequately insured.**

CHAPTER 13

Staring Down the Unexpected

Prime Spending Years

Sure, you're earning more. But, if you're like most people, you're probably spending more, too, because you have a lot more responsibility, including providing for a retirement that's getting ever closer. Meanwhile, you've reached a point in your life when you feel you deserve to spend a little more money on yourself, and to think pretty seriously about leaving all that work behind. Maybe you feel like going a little crazy on that sports car while you can still enjoy it.

Well, for Starters, There's Downsizing

Cutting reality down to size

With big responsibilities at your door, and without the right financial planning to cushion the blow, downsizing could force you down and maybe even out, despite your prime earning potential. The days when you could expect long-term loyalty from a company and an automatic career ladder from day one to retirement are gone. You, or someone you know, have probably had your first brush with downsizing, restructuring, or "redundancy." Your age group has been hardest hit by this downsizing trend: middle management is the first to go in a large company. This can be frightening, especially if you've lived your life on the assumption that once you started working, you would be working for life, and seeing a steady increase in income.

What this means for you

Start by looking at your industry and your company. Is your industry growing or shrinking? If you are working in the telecommunications industry, for example, and the industry is growing, you will have less to worry about than someone in a shrinking industry. If you think you are a target for downsizing, a few outcomes are possible:

- You could lose your job. This is the worst case scenario. If that happens, you will have to decide what you want to do next, and you will want to have saved enough money to tide you over if your severance package or EI runs out.
- You could be forced into early retirement. This will also take a bite out of your lifestyle, but the damage can be minimized if you're prepared.
- You could beat downsizing before it beats you. That means doing everything in your power either to hold on to your job, to strike out on your own, to retire or semi-retire in comfort, or maybe even to start a second career.

What you do will depend on a number of factors: you and your partner's goals, your present and future financial situation and responsibilities, and also, your personality. Starting your own business isn't for everyone. The point is, you now have a lot of freedom to change

PRIME TIME EARNERS:
SINGLE INCOME MEANS DOUBLE THE RISK

Raising a family, being downsized, and retiring early are all factors that can reduce your family to a single income. If you are now the only income earner in your family you want to be doubly sure that you are prepared for anything unexpected. Plan to save more money for emergencies and make sure you are covered by insurance — both disability and life.

careers or jobs. This may become more and more valuable to you as your personal and family goals change.

Plan for downsizing

The present downsizing climate could mean you could lose your pension, and even your savings, if you can't find a job right away. That's why it's more important than ever to have a backup plan if your job doesn't work out. If one of you isn't working, you will have to do a bit more contingency planning than the average family. These are just a few of the things you can do to minimize the blow of downsizing:

- Put your financial house in order now, and make a plan for how you will use a severance package and pension benefits, if you get them.
- Create an emergency fund. The size of this depends on your income and your responsibilities. Three months' salary is usual.
- Take out a line of credit. Do this while you are still working — you'll have a hard time convincing the bank to give you a line of credit when you don't have any income.

Benefit from Your Benefits

If you are not a salaried employee, look into setting up your own benefits plan, especially if you have children. Some professional associations offer benefit plans to members. Insurance companies now offer packages that add health, dental, and disability insurance to public health insurance. These packages make insurance more affordable for you. Examine your average annual health costs and compare them to the cost of monthly insurance payments to get a sense of whether you would benefit from the blanket protection of insurance.

Health care

This is an area of prime concern as you become a more likely candidate for health complications. Take a good look at your company's plan. Does it include spousal coverage? Coverage for common-law or same-sex partners? Children? What, precisely, does it cover — how much per operation, how much per child, dental for the family or just you? Write down a specific list of what you need covered ("everything" won't do) and compare it with the statement of company insurance policy. Once you have identified the gaps, take your list to an insurance agent you trust (this is important — it's all too easy to come home with more than what you need or want) and look for the most comprehensive policy available. Finally, don't depend on anything from the provincial or federal governments. Keep your health card up to date, to be sure, and make sure all of your dependants have one, but cover the gaps in a company plan with your own insurance, if you can.

Pension

Although most pension benefits end if you leave the company, you may be able to take a taxable cash settlement or transfer your benefits to another plan or to an RRSP. Ask for professional help in assessing your options when your employment ends.

Employment Insurance (EI)

Employment Insurance is the new, more positive name for Unemployment Insurance, the government program that provides employees with a percentage of their income while they are searching for a new position. If you received a severance package, your Employment Insurance will start only when your severance runs out. Your EI also may be reduced if your severance was equal to more than 52 weeks' pay. Your eligibility may depend on the type and length of your employment and the number of weeks that you work a year. Many positions have long periods of off-time, which can affect eligibility. For example, university teaching assistants and fishery workers have had their EI benefits withheld on the basis that they know when they will be unemployed and so can set up other work for their down times. Because EI can be unexpectedly complicated, you should go to the EI office immediately, even if you think you'll be unemployed for only a short time.

Severance

Severance is compensation for being terminated without cause and without adequate notice. Like pensions and other benefits, severance is usually available only to salaried employees and it varies greatly in

PRIME-TIME EARNERS

The larger your severance, the longer you'll have to wait for employment insurance.

amount. There are minimum requirements for severance pay in lieu of notice, which vary between provinces.

Severance is fully taxable in the year that it is received. In some cases, part of the severance may be transferred to an RRSP, depending on how many years of service prior to 1996 you had with the employer. It's a good idea to sit down and talk to your financial advisor about these options as soon as you can. If your company offers any financial planning assistance (many large companies do when they restructure staff), take advantage of it.

Plan Ahead for Unemployment

Planning to lose your job may seem like a hobby for a pessimist, but being prepared is always a good idea. Again, make sure that you have an emergency fund built into your budget. Emergency funds are important for everyone, but they are essential for homeowners, parents of children, or people with financial responsibilities, such as payments on a car loan. You might arrange a line of credit, which provides a loan that you can use at any time if you think your unemployment might be short term (see Chapter 9). Or you could invest in a money market mutual fund, where your money will be quickly

HOW MUCH IS ENOUGH?

Depending on your situation, your emergency fund should hold the equivalent of at least three months' income. If your job is fairly stable and you have family and friends who can help you out in times of need, three months' income should suffice. But if you are self-employed or in a volatile field, you may need more — perhaps twelve months' income stashed away as insurance against dry periods.

accessible should you need it. What you don't want to do is cash in your RRSP unless you absolutely have to. Not only will you have to pay taxes on the investments you withdraw, but you cannot re-contribute the amounts that you have withdrawn.

Don't Lose It If You Lose Your Job

Losing a job can be terrifying and embarrassing, but it can also be your chance to change positions to your advantage. This may be the event that leads to something better. If you've established good savings habits, you've got at least a three-month cushion to fall back on.

Use this time to think about what you really want to do. If you were in a job that you were unsuited for, think about why that job didn't fit you and evaluate your skills. Perhaps your former position didn't challenge you to do what you are good at. Consider your other options. This might be a good time to go back to school for that degree you always wanted. Or maybe you think you can finally start your own business at home. Job counselling can help you decide what to do next.

Make a Plan of Action

- Minimize the tax you'll have to pay on your severance package.
- Minimize the tax you'll have to pay on your pension benefits by taking advantage of roll-overs where available.

TIGHTENING YOUR BELT

Just in case, here are a few budgeting tips on how to live with a reduced income.

- Take stock of your spending habits. Try to reduce discretionary spending to a minimum: avoid the drycleaners, eat at home.
- Assess your fixed expenses. Take more time to find better deals on the things you must buy.
- Reduce your financial responsibilities. Is it time to end your car lease? Move into a smaller place? Take in a boarder?
- Defer contributions to your RRSP or your savings plan.

- Start a new budget.
- Don't pay your bills before they are due.

Work to Reward Yourself

In today's employment world, you have both greater opportunities and higher risks than ever before. Make the best of your situation by planning carefully, thinking about your goals and how you can meet them, and enlisting the help of financial and industry experts to give you a realistic forecast of your needs. You are in charge, and you should work as hard for yourself by planning ahead as you would for any employer. With a little bit of introspection, planning, and bravery, you can have the working life you want.

What If the Golden Handshake Comes Early?

A lot of people are choosing to retire early. If you're one of them, then you've already put a plan in place to make it possible. But what if you're one of those whom retirement finds first? It could be because of downsizing, the economy, or changes in your industry. You can't prepare for everything, but if you're caught unawares by sudden retirement, don't panic. Find someone who can advise you on the right steps to take.

Summary

Not all surprises are nice: the reality of life in the workplace is that you might find yourself on the receiving end of someone else's problems. Being where you are in your life, you might be more likely to get the early golden handshake (or the golden boot) because middle management is often the first to go in "restructurings." There's no point to living in fear of these kinds of upsets, though, especially if you make the pre-emptive strike of being prepared. Know how your various benefits can help you in times of need, and in the case of an unforeseen opportunity to change, remember that it's up to you to see it all as new horizons rather than shattered dreams.

QUICK RECAP

1. **Be aware of what direction your industry and your company is going in, and use this awareness to plan for possible change.**
2. **Use and create emergency resources. Benefits of all sorts can be used to see yourself through tough times, and an emergency fund can make the difference between panicking or having time to change direction.**
3. **Remember that every ending is a beginning: the end of one phase of your work life (willed or not) is an opportunity to start something new and exciting.**

CHAPTER 14

Going for Gold

Get ready to enjoy the rest of your life. Now that you've read this far, you know that financial planning isn't half as intimidating as you once thought. And that your dreams can be realized. Congratulations! This knowledge puts you far ahead of many people who are too afraid to begin even thinking about their finances and their retirement, let alone take charge of them. Until this stage in your life, you may have got by without putting much planning into how to keep your households running, like Maggie, Shelly and John, and Gord and Beth. But you, like them, want to do more than just get by — you want to be able to retire comfortably, with the freedom to do what you want. That doesn't mean you have to tighten your belt to the point that you can no longer breathe. It's just means taking time to take stock of where you are and where you want to go. Then you can start making the smart decisions to get there. Planning for your retirement should become part of your life, don't let it take over your life.

The whole point of financial health is to follow a few sensible steps to become financially secure enough to live the way you want to. It's up to you when you retire and how much you save for your retirement. You may want to keep working for a few more years so that your years of retirement really will be golden, not tin. Maybe you'll never make it to the St. Andrew's golf course in Scotland, but you may make it down to one of Florida's better ones. Then again, starting now instead of a year from now will make it likely you can get to Scotland. Anything is possible.

Start by Helping Yourself

A trained financial advisor is best equipped to help you plan for your retirement. Take as much advice as you can. But the trick is to also rely on yourself, your instincts, and your desires. You know better than anyone else what you need and what you want. Others can help you plan, choose between investment options, and better understand available strategies, but they can't do it all. Your money and your welfare matters most to you, and you, ultimately, are the best caretaker of your future.

If you have a spouse or partner, talk to them about what they see in their future and your future together. You may find your visions differ slightly, but it's better to find that out now, rather than when they head off to Capetown to do development work while you are left teeing off alone. Once you both know what you want, revisit your list of assets, liabilities, and savings goals.

Determine what you have to do now, if anything, to make the present more enjoyable and your upcoming retirement worry free. If your main problem is your RRSP — or lack thereof — then take a look at your budget and decide how you can start devoting more of it to your retirement savings. Don't be afraid to ask for help from friends and your financial advisor.

Get into a Routine

Even if you haven't followed an investment regimen in the past, you now have the knowledge and the power to begin. The key to your continued financial health is to be aware of your financial situation and make financial planning part of your regular routine. If you put this advice into practice, you will witness your net worth grow into a comfortable nest egg for your retirement. You are ready to start taking action. You wouldn't expect to lose weight by sitting on a sofa watching Jane Fonda do aerobics for you; nor should you expect that good intentions without action will get your finances in order. Start today!

ONE MORE TIME

As we told you in Chapter 1, the key to sound financial management and a secure financial future is to assess your situation regularly. Here's a review:

At least once a year, assess your financial situation as well as your long-term and short-term financial goals. Establish a realistic and comfortable plan to achieve those goals. Implement your plan, keeping in mind your risk tolerance and time horizon. Use a financial advisor the same way you would use a doctor — take advantage of their expertise to ensure your financial health.

It's easy. Think of it as your annual review. Don't forget to consider the following:

- net worth
- budget
- will
- retirement goals
- investment portfolio
- insurance needs

General Summary

1. Do a self-assessment and re-prioritize your goals.
2. Make plans for where and how you want to live during your retirement.
3. Determine how much annual income you will need to support your desired lifestyle in your retirement.
4. Assess your net worth at least annually.
5. Manage your debt. Be sure to get rid of your debt before you retire.
6. When buying big assets, consider how they will affect your retirement plans.
7. Review your risk tolerance and adjust your investment portfolio accordingly.
8. Maximize your RRSP contributions to maximize your tax savings.
9. Make sure both spouses are involved in the financial plan, so that either could carry on alone if the other spouse dies or there is a marriage breakdown.
10. Review your estate plan regularly.

Then, sit back and enjoy!

Index